TAROT

MIRROR OF THE SOUL

TAROT

MIRROR OF THE SOUL

**Handbook for the
Aleister Crowley Tarot**

Gerd Ziegler

WEISER BOOKS
San Francisco, CA / Newburyport, MA

First published in 1988 by
Red Wheel/Weiser, LLC
With offices at
665 Third Street, Suite 400
San Francisco, CA 94107
www.redwheelweiser.com

ISBN: 978-0-87728-683-7

Library of Congress Cataloging-in-Publication Data
Ziegler, Gerd.
         Tarot : mirror of the soul.

         1. Tarot. I. Title.
BF1879.T2Z54   1988   133.3'2424   87-34087

Printed in Canada
MP
20 19 18 17

CONTENTS

FOREWORD

Just as we use a mirror to observe our exterior, we can use the images of the Tarot to approach our inner reality. An adventurous expedition! The images of the Tarot are a mirror of the images in our souls. The longer we look inward, the more we discover about ourselves and our lives.

A mirror reflects visible reality without judging it. It shows the beautiful and the ugly, the pleasant and the unpleasant. It cannot do anything else. We can put it aside or shatter it if we don't like our reflection, but doing so won't change our appearance.

The images of the Tarot describe spiritual conditions. In using the cards we see our inner reality from new perspectives. The images are neither »positive« nor »negative«, neither »for« nor »against« us. They simply offer hints and clues. We can examine them, choosing either to discard or consider, ignore or use them.

Many people are afraid to confront their inner reality; they may find ugly or unpleasant aspects of themselves. They pretend to know themselves, often believing they really do. They expend enormous amounts of energy in maintaining an illusory facade; the more illusory, the more desperately they defend it and the greater their underlying fear. Yet each defensive action, each denial, reveals, rather than hides, the underlying insecurity. Fear, narrow-mindedness, repression, constriction and a sense of isolation result, and the true inner reality remains unknown.

Surprisingly, we learn to accept and love ourselves only when we stop trying to hide, and hide from, our inner reality. We can only share with others those parts of ourselves which we had discovered and accepted, and can only change those unpleasant aspects in ourselves which we have thoroughly examined, and recognized as needing change.

Self-exploration can be risky at times. Newly-won perspectives can upset old habits and attitudes, and shake the very foundation of our belief systems (see The Tower). Yet this is an essential step in any transformational process.

The »rewards« of such an internal cleansing process are great. Each time we reveal and let go of one of our illusions, we come one step closer to our own true, boundless and enduring selves. What we let go and lose in this process never has been really ours; what is destroyed never has been rooted in our true being.

In letting go you arrive at the still place in yourself where you and the stillness are one; you arrive home and you and your home are one.

This book offers suggestions for playing with and increasing your understanding of the Crowley-Thoth Tarot. It will help you in your work with the cards, sometimes guiding your inner exploration, sometimes pointing the way in daily situations and difficult decision-making processes.

Tarot means, above all, subjectivity, and maintaining a vital readiness to being touched. The Tarot's images, as mirrors of our own unconscious impulses, unlock and make these impulses available to our conscious mind. And we learn to interpret the messages of the cards, as we might interpret a muddled dream, we can discover new inner realms, and gain a glimpse into the mysteries of the Universe in its all-encompassing cosmic order.

Waakirchen, August 1984
Zolling, July 1985

THE SYSTEM
OF THE TAROT

The Tarot is an ancient system of knowledge which has been taught over the centuries in secret Mystery schools. This wisdom is presented through paintings, the symbols often hidden in esoteric images. Each card embodies the energy of the symbols on it, reflecting and imparting that energy to the user of the deck. The Tarot was originally a book of wisdom, similar to the Chinese *I Ging*, and was looked to for advice in many different matters.

The Tarot is a tool that can be used for orienting oneself on the path toward greater awareness, – a vast path with many turnings. It is a guide to the realm of inner transformation, revealing hidden messages and enlarging one's vision of the self and the cosmos. We can use the Tarot as a map, drawn in symbols, indicating the roadsigns on the inner path. Correctly used, it gives insight and new perspectives about any unclear situations. It possesses intense transformatory power which can lead to valuable breakthroughs, increased clarity and deeper perceptions regarding areas of life which are most meaningful to us. If we are ready to see and accept, the Tarot will give us information that points to special strengths as well as uncovering blind spots.

The 78 cards are divided into 22 Major Arcana (numbered 0–XXI), 16 Court Cards and 40 Minor Arcana.

Major Arcana cards give us answers or messages regarding the question or situation at hand. At the same time, they offer higher universal teachings based in Cosmic Law. These teachings provide an answer to the immediate question, while also providing a lesson which can be generally applied in every-day life.

Court Cards generally are related in some way to people who are important in our lives. They show us also what we have to learn and what we wish to master, as well as any special talents we may have.

Minor Arcana cards concern the smaller, more direct lessons of life. They are divided into 4 suits, with ten cards in each. The suits are:

Wands, ruled by the element Fire. These cards stand for energy in general, especially sexual energy (the Yang or male aspect), perception, intuition, insight and activity.

Cups, ruled by the element Water. These reflect our inner emotional reality. Their realm includes love, feelings, interaction in relationships and sexual energy (the Yin, or feminine aspect).

Swords, ruled by the element Air. Cards of the Sword suit generally reflect our spiritual or mental condition, processes or attitudes, including possibly, meditation processes. This level of our being is most susceptible to disturbance. We are repeatedly challenged to prove that what we have achieved on this plane is real. The Sword cards also show us what energies we are using (usually unconsciously) to shape our lives.

Disks, ruled by the element Earth. These indicate our external, material, physical reality. The external mirrors the internal. Dealings with the earth realm include health, the body, nutrition, clothing, possessions, finances, poverty and wealth.

THE CROWLEY-THOTH TAROT

The creation of this Tarot deck has its roots in the activities of the Hermetic Order of the Golden Dawn, an English Rosicrucian society which Aleister Crowley joined in 1898. The Order offered a systematic and clear approach to the Mystery Traditions. It is said that one of the goals of the Order was the transformation of Western social systems through its work with symbolism and ancient wisdom.

Aleister Crowley's life's work was an attempt to extract and unify the essential Truth of all the traditional schools of Wisdom and religions, and make that Truth available in one complete system to help modern Humanity in the search for God-realization and Oneness.

Crowley originally intended his deck to be a correction and updating of the classic medieval Tarot. He planned to spend three months working on the designs which Frieda Harris would then paint. Instead, the project grew into a deep exploration and integration of the esoteric symbolism of different traditions of Ancient Wisdom. The work lasted five years and was one of Crowley's last projects before he died in 1947. Crowley wrote at one time that it was only through the dedication and genius of Harris, who was herself an Egyptologist, that he became more and more deeply involved in the evolution and creation of a wholly new deck. Harris worked from Crowley's rough sketches or verbal descriptions, and although she was not very familiar with the Tarot herself, her intuitive understanding and knowledge influenced and complemented Crowley's ideas. She often painted a card repeatedly until she was satisfied. There are 1200 symbols included in the 78 cards. The most commonly occurring ones are described in the last part of this book.

Neither Crowley nor Harris (who died in 1962) managed to publish the deck during their lifetimes. In 1969, Major Grady L. McMurtry, who had helped Crowley publish *The Book of Thoth* in 1944, had the paintings photographed and published.

THE USE
OF THE TAROT

Drawing a Card from the Deck

The drawing of a Tarot card should always be preceded by a small
ritual. When turning to the Tarot for guidance in important questions,
give the moment a beautiful, meditative flavor. Keep the cards in a
special box or wrapped in a beautiful cloth of one solid color. Shuffle
the cards carefully in an attitude of stillness, and then fan them out on
the cloth. A candle, incense, flowers, the picture of a beloved person
or any other personal object lends a special and ceremonial flavor to
the proceedings.

Before drawing any cards, shake your hands briefly (or if necessary
more energetically) to relax any tension and allow the energy to flow
more easily. You will always use the left hand, the one related to the
unconscious and intuitive side of the brain, for drawing the cards.

The next important consideration is the question which you want the
Tarot to answer. The wisdom which lives in each of us has been lost
in great part to the conscious mind, and can be rediscovered in the
process of working with the Tarot. Questions asked of the cards are
questions asked of our own unconscious. The more definite and precise
your questions are, the better the Tarot will be able to function as a
clear mirror of your inner wisdom. Before and while drawing a card,
your eyes may be closed. Some people find the cards visually, however.
The breath flows gently and deeply to the heart, and the consciousness
is directed fully toward the question. Now just trust the hand that seeks
the card!

The most important factor in understanding the images is your first,
spontaneous reaction. Only after you are genuinely aware of these
should you look to the book for further assistance. Here you may find
suggestions which will give you a fuller understanding of the symbols.

At the end of each explanation you will find more »personal« hints, questions, suggestions and affirmations, which are intended as guides for your own further work with the Tarot. If the questions and suggestions do not apply exactly to your own situation, you can use them as patterns, if needed, for devising your own. Affirmations are life-affirmative, positive statements of self-acceptance which make us aware of any self-limiting ideas, feelings of resistance or negative patterns. Repeating affirmations aloud daily to ourselves helps replace these old negative beliefs which prevent our change and growth.

Why This Card?

When discussing the drawing of a particular card, it may help to consider the concept of synchronicity. This expression was coined by C. G. Jung, who made a life's work of studying archetypal images and symbols of the mind. In his years of study and experimentation with the Chinese *Book of Changes (I Ging)*, he repeatedly came up against a phenomenon which he called synchronicity. Synchronicity, by no means fully researched at this time, is the apparently inexplicable co-incidence of events which cannot be logically proven to be connected.

We all know about coincidence from our own experience. For example, you are just about to phone a friend when the phone rings and it's your friend calling you. Or you read in the newspaper about a big fire that happened in the night and realize you had a dream about a burning house at the time of the fire. When you turn on the TV to see a football game, suddenly you know, without knowing how, which team will win, and it does. The examples are endless.

The knowledge necessary for understanding such phenomena is for the most part lost to us. Sometimes the messages coming from within seem encoded in ways which make their meanings indecipherable to us. The Tarot can be used as a key to the images and conditions of our spiritual realms. The paintings on each card you draw from the deck reflect an aspect of your interior at the moment you pick the card.

When we carry the principle of synchronicity further, it means that our entire perception of the exterior world, the totality of our experience, is synchronized with our interior. In this case, each person creates his or her own reality anew every moment. If you recognize and accept this, you are ready to take full responsibility for yourself and your life.

The pictures and symbols of the Tarot play the role of a go-between. The same card will have totally different meanings for different people, and even different meanings for the same person at different points in time, in different situations. The card you draw reveals something about your mental/spiritual condition and energy at the moment you are drawing the card. The card expresses and bears the energy of the symbols on it. These are synchronous with your own energies. As your hand, a channel for your energy, moves above the cards, it will be drawn to the card with the corresponding (synchronous) energy.

How to Meet the Tarot

Everyone who plays Tarot decides personally what meaning this picture-book of wisdom has for her or him. This is revealed by the attitude, the outlook with which we approach the cards. Is it pure curiosity? Scepticism? Readiness to experiment? Whatever our conscious motives are, it is important to meet the cards playfully and with humor, never in deadly earnest. The Tarot reminds us again and again that life is a play, and is to be lived playfully no matter how serious our situation may seem or how identified we may feel with the conditions facing us. Tarot helps us see the world with a certain distance. It teaches us to see from different perspectives, and with a broader vision.

If you are prepared to accept and approach the Tarot as an advisor, come with openness and loving respect, as you would to a good, wise friend. It will then be possible to develop vital, intimate communication with it. You will never cease to be amazed by the directness with which the Tarot answers, laying open obscure or hidden aspects of your life.

The highest goal of working with cards is an ever-growing trust in the perceptions from our inner reality, learning to hear the voice of our own hearts, discovering our own inner guide.

The Art of Asking Questions

The quality of the question you ask the Tarot determines the quality of the answer you receive. Some examples follow that will help you learn the art of formulating questions.

Questions about the here and now
   I am drawing a card to represent me at this time and place.
   What is my inner reality now?
   What is my present situation?
   What is influencing me strongly at this time?
   What surrounds me?
   How should I behave?
The Tarot will give answers to any questions asked about your present situation. Of course the above questions are only model-frameworks to be filled out more specifically depending on your individual condition. It is best to ask no more than three questions at a time. You should also aware, before asking, of just how ready you are to hear the answer given, it may be less flattering to your ego than you would like. Remember that the Tarot is there to help us out of ruts, to help us see beyond the limitations we may have lived within until now, and to help broaden our view of reality.

Making Decisions
A decision that concerns you may involve simple, everyday banalities, or deeper, more life-shattering alternatives. When looking to the Tarot for assistance in reaching a decision, consider your readiness to accept information and make use of the hints which may provide clear, if unexpected, direction. If the cards are repeatedly misused, that is to say, if important messages are repeatedly ignored, they will soon lose power and cease to give you clear answers.
   If the decision to be made could be solved in several different ways it is best to be clear, before asking the Tarot, what these are, and what the possible outcomes of each alternative are. Only draw cards for alternatives that you would truly choose. It is nonsense to draw a card for an alternative you would not really consider.
   Example 1: I have a career choice to make. I can either a) engage myself more fully in my present position, or b) give it up and be free for something totally new. I will draw a card for each possibility, and am ready to take the suggestions the Tarot shows me.
   The Tarot's answer: for possibility a) Five of Cups (Disappointment) and for possibility b) Ace of Disks (also see the description of card, but it generally stands for inner and outer riches). In this case the Tarot has decided obviously for b). this is a hint to be open to a change in career.
   Example 2: My relationship with X has been very tense for quite a while. Would a) a parting of the ways be more helpful now or should we b) remain in the relationship and spend more time »having it out,« to release the tension?

The Tarot's answer: for a) Eight of Cups (Indolence) and for b) Prince of Wands (also see the description, but it generally stands for moving out of darkness into the light). Here the Tarot shows clearly that a parting of the ways is flight from a potentially fruitful interaction.

Questions about the past

Questions about the past often testify to unresolved relationships and/or situations we have not worked through. The Tarot can be used to help clarify and resolve such unfinished questions. The final question in such a session should relate to the effect of the former learning experience on your present situation. Some sample questions are:

What am I holding on to?

What was there for me to learn in that relationship/situation?

What was I avoiding?

What can I do now to resolve the unfinished?

Questions about the future

These are probably the most popular questions, but they are also the most trickly to ask. Choose these especially carefully, and look critically at what lies behind the question for you. The Tarot generally refuses to answer questions asked out of sheer curiosity, or those asked when you are unwilling to take responsibility for the events in your life. This is not to say that questions about the future are taboo. I believe there is much to be said for the idea that the future is available to us at every moment, just as the events of the past are available through memory. The Tarot can be helpful in advising about upcoming situations.

Example 1: You will soon be meeting with an important person. Possible questions you might ask include:

What significance does the relationship with this person have for me?

What significance does this meeting have for our relationship?

What is this person bringing me?

How should I behave with him/her?

What can I learn in dealing with this person?

Example 2: A task of some sort (test, business, a decision, journey, etc.). Possible questions might be:

What does this event mean for my life?

What will happen if I engage myself totally (avoid totally)?

What life lesson can I learn through this event?

What are my greatest hopes and fears?

How should I meet this task?

Questions about people not present
It is perfectly legitimate to ask questions in order to clarify relationships with people who are not present, or to ask for information about people we feel special bonds with. We do this daily in our thoughts. However, it is always best to ask the cards first if this is the proper time to set up contact with the person concerned, and if the cards are ready to give information about this person. If the Tarot affirms these basic questions, you may put your consciousness in contact with the chosen person, and let the question come which you wish to ask. Holding this question, you draw a card and receive the answer.

THE
MAJOR ARCANA

0 THE FOOL

Key Words: *openness, trust; ready to take a risk; courage to stand your ground; freedom, independence; creativity; great potential; possibility to take a quantum leap; listening to the heart's voice.*

The Fool is represented by the god of Spring, Dionysus. The green color reminds us of the powerful creative force of Spring. The crocodile (the ancient Egyptian god of creativity) is also the bearer of the greatest creative powers.

The long umbilical cord, connection to cosmic oneness, wraps the Fool in four spirals. The possibility of rebirth is given on all four planes of human existence: spiritual, intellectual, emotional and physical. The prerequisite is your readiness to change in all areas; your responsibility to self-development.

The four spirals are described as follows:

The first spiral surrounds the heart in heart-shape. It stands for emotional rebirth; the recognition, perception and acceptance of true emotional needs.

The second spiral bears three symbols. The dove represents vulnerability and sensitivity as requirements for love of oneself and others. The ability to set limits and say »No« in unclear relationships is also needed. The butterfly means transformation (the caterpillar becomes the butterfly). The snakes wrapped arround each other (Caduceus) are a symbol for engagement in in healing and health.

On **the third spiral** lay two naked children entwined. Their presence brings the realm of relationship into the picture. The quality of your relationships with family, friends, business associates and deep emotional bonds must be re-examined and re-evaluated. Which people do you really want around you?

The fourth spiral is occupied by the tiger and the crocodile. The crocodile urges for the development of creative abilities in work and career. The rose it wears symbolizes the unfolding of creative powers. The crocodile's powerful jaws testify to its endurance and leadership qualities, as well as to the, ability to work independently and self-sufficiently. It is possible to break through old, worn-out conditioning.

The tiger symbolizes fear (see Princess of Wands). Dionysus is repeatedly bitten by this tiger, but his gaze remains directed forward. He gives no attention to fear, so it has lost its power over him. The tiger cannot injure him at all. His unshakable faith in existence allows him to be aware of fearful feelings without being their victim. He is liberated, able to be receptive for mystical peak experiences and interpersonal interaction. Basic, dynamic powers are released which drive forward. The onrushing creative unfolding process cannot be held back.

The Fool holds a cup with a base of crystal in his right hand and a burning torch in his left. These are alchemical symbols (see the card XIV Art). They show the meeting of opposite forces which creates the energy for the transformation, the quantum leap, to take place.

The grapes, symbols of fertility, are ripe for harvest. The white spots on the golden background mean Fall (harvest time); falling leaves, dropping, letting go, surrender. The coins at the right, engraved with astrological symbols, reflect the overflowing wealth on all planes which comes when you give your creative energies full rein to unfold.

The horns Dionysus wears reflect expanded perception. The rainbow surrounding his head means wholeness, Unity, the bridge between heaven and earth, inner and outer. Between his legs is a cluster of flowers which represents the process of tranformation. At the bottom, the active aspect (the three flowers to the left symbolize body, mind and spirit) combines with the passive aspect, receptivity, willingness to learn. The simple blossoms below, when united, give birth to the many-petalled blossom above.

The sun symbolizes the creative and transformatory powers released by the melting of basic sexual energy.

Indications: *You are ready for a new beginning, perhaps even a quantum leap. Give in, dare to leap, even if fear attempts to hold you back. Trust the voice from within your heart.*

Questions: *What is the »tiger of fear« for you? How do you imagine the courageous leap into the new? What does it look like? Where does your heart call you to go?*

Suggestion: *Draw other cards for the above questions if their answers are not clear for you.*

Affirmation: *I now follow my heart. I am open, and ready to go wherever it may lead me.*

I THE MAGUS

Key Words: *Mercury; communication; playful dealings with all possible forms of communication; flexibility, brilliance.*

The Magus is represented by the Greek god Mercury, the messenger with wings of pure spirit (see the yellow wings on his feet). Mercury bears energy which spreads and radiates from him. The cards represents the Will, Wisdom and the Word through which the world was created.

Mercury balances with great skill on the tip of a surfboard-shaped stand and juggles with the different tools of communication. He is a genius at using all the possibilities available to him.

In his duality, Mercury stands for truth and falsehood. He brings all set ideas and judgements into question, which often makes him appear in a questionable light himself. As a creative creature, he knows no conscience. He uses all tools, all methods, to arrive at his goal. The temptation to misuse his talents is great. His ability and skill lend him superiority and power. He moves on the narrow border between white and black magic. This means he needs constant self-examination. He can use his talents in a self-seeking manner, or in the service of love and light.

In this painting, the Magus plays with the possiblities of communication. he wears a smile, meaning that he communicates with humor. The humorous playful ease with which he manipulates his ability is an indication of its potential positive use. The monkey is the companion of the Egyptian god of Wisdom, Thoth. He illustrates that wisdom can never be regulated in set ways. Any external manifestation, for example through words, includes in it some illusion.

The objects Mercury juggles represent different realms of communication. For example:

1. Coins: body, matter, finance.
2. Fire: inspiration, transformation, dynamics.
3. Wand: philosophy, religion, spirituality.
4. Arrow: directness, honesty, purposefulness.
5. Scroll: writing, publication.
6. Winged Egg: extra-sensory perception, telepathy.
7. Cup with Snake: emotions, relationships, sexuality.
8. Sword: intellect, logic, analysis.

The two snakes at his head are an ancient Egyptian symbol for healing and regeneration (Caduceus). In this context they refer to the regeneration of thought. Above them is the Eye of Horus (god of Perception) with the symbol of a dove (bearer of the spirit). The Magus receives inspiration from the soul of the Universe whose message he spreads on Earth. This is more strongly expressed by the blue/yellow energy-beam which enters his head, penetrates through his body, and emerges again at his feet.

He cannot fulfill his tasks without constantly remaining in touch with the spiritual forces of the universe. He is always in the service of a superior law. When he recognizes and accepts this as his true function, he bears clarifying light into the darkness of ignorance and misunderstanding.

Indications: *You have at your disposal brilliant capabilities which you should share with other people. One important task is to find or create the proper surroundings for your activities.*

Questions: *In what areas lie your talents? With what methods, and in what surroundings can you pass them on or share them?*

Suggestion: *Visualize your ideal area of activity. Describe it.*

Affirmation: *The full expression of my creative potential fulfills me and makes me happy and satisfied.*

II THE PRIESTESS

Key Words: *Moon; access to intuitive powers, healing, independence, inner equilibrium, increased self-confidence.*

The Priestess is represented by the Moon-goddess Isis. She is surrounded by a fine network of light rays, an expression of her spiritual nature. Her essence is unrestricted independence.

She is in touch with her intuitive abilities, and can trust them completely. She perceives and is connected with her own inner voice, the internal guide and healer. This shows outwardly in her trust in and responsibility to herself. Like the camel, which can travel long stretches in the desert without water, you, when you have discovered your own inner spring, also radiate a satisfied sense of self-sufficiency. You find fertile oases (flowers and fruits at the bottom of the card) in the innermost reaches of your being. The more you accept yourself and share with others, the deeper the clarity of your perceptions will become (represented by the crystals).

In this deck, the Priestess is one of the strongest cards for balance, equilibrium and harmony. The upper half of her body expresses the feminine-receptive. This is accented by the upward-swinging lines and the upward-pointing crescent-moons behind her head. The crown is the Moon which receives light from the Sun.

From the navel down, her body expresses the male principle. The lines are straight, dynamic, direct in purpose. The bow and arrow in her lap accentuate this concept.

The Priestess can indicate extra-sensory perception and intuitive abilities, such as clairvoyance, telepathy, creative visualization, empathy, intuitive knowledge, and healing powers. These abilities arise in harmony with, and in service to, the ultimate cosmic laws.

Indications: *You now have access to your intuitive powers. Develop them more fully. Guard your independence!*

Question: *Are there areas in your life in which you allow others to influence you rather than trusting your own intuition?*

Suggestion: *Seek out water as often as you can. Meditate near water, and learn from it as much as you can.*

Affirmation: *I trust my intuitive abilities.*

III THE EMPRESS

ל The Empress ♀

Key Words: *Venus; beauty; love; motherliness; femininity; wisdom; connection between spirit and matter; inner and outer wealth.*

The Empress embodies and commands the feminine in all its forms. Her form and surroundings are marked by beauty and wholeness. You feel a sense of well-being in her presence, taking part in the harmony of her being. Her beauty is not restricted only to the externally visible. Her femininity is fully evolved on all levels of her being, given her a special radiance. She is mother and lover, ruler and seer at the same time. Her strength rests in the unifying of the highest spiritual values in their fully perceivable forms, with the lowest material qualities.

The essential characteristics of her dominion are love in its giving and its receptive aspects (white and red), creativity and fruitfulness (green), understanding and wisdom (blue). Her right hand holds the phallus-like stem of the lotus which unfolds its petals in front of her heart chakra. Her left hand is open receptively. The creativity of male procreative power unifies itself with femal surrender. After she has integrated the male aspects of herself, a woman will be internally and externally in harmony.

The pink-white pelican which feeds its brood with its own blood signifies unconditional mother-love, nourishing the young with its whole being. The Empress also represents the Great Mother, Mother Earth, who gives birth to and nourishes all living beings.

The double-headed white eagle on the shield (corresponding with the red eagle of The Emperor) symbolizes the transformation which arises through the unification of the diverse aspects of your being.

Moon and Earth are united and surrounded by a magnetic energy field. When the emotional depths of the unconscious (Moon) manifest visibly (Earth), they become available for consciousness to use (blue flames to the right and left). When the powers from within are integrated, you will radiate wholeness and completeness which attracts other people magnetically because it gives them a feeling of security and protection to be in your presence. The union of Moon and Earth appears once again on the crown. The Maltese Cross emphasizes the significance of the union between spiritual and material.

Her face is turned toward the dove, she is oriented toward the future. In her wisdom, she has turned from the past, the sparrow.

The opening in the arch behind her can be seen as a gateway to heaven. This beautiful physical form merely hints at something more beautiful, much greater, which is hidden in it. Hermann Hesse described »every phenomenon on earth as an image, saying that all images are open gates through which the soul can enter the inner world when it is ready. Here you and I and everything else are all one. Every person comes to such an open gate at some time in life, but few go through the gate or give up the pretty illusions on this side for what we may sense lies within the reality of the inner.«*

Indications: *The beauty you see in others which attracts you to them is a beauty you carry within yourself. You are in the process of unfolding and evolving your femininity. This may be the right time to work through and clarify unresolved mother-conflicts.*

Question: *In your life is there a beautiful, strong woman from whom you would like to learn?*

Suggestion: *Visualize your ideal woman! Write down her most important qualities. Try to find these in others and yourself. Surround yourself with beauty and abundance.*

Affirmation: *I am filled with power and beauty.*

---

* Hermann Hesse, *Die Märchen*, »Iris«; Suhrkamp 291, Frankfurt/Main

IV THE EMPEROR

Key Words: *Aries; pioneer, discoverer, leader, initiator; creative wisdom; great leadership qualities; urge for action, adventurousness, new beginning; fatherhood, authority.*

The Emperor is portrayed as a crowned man in a majestic gown. The globe with the Maltese Cross (symbol of imperial dignity) represents the unification of wisdom and worldly mastery.

His throne, which glows with the fiery colors of Mars and the Sun, is ornamented with the heads of wild Himalayan rams. His scepter also bears this symbol of power and adventurousness. the reclining lamb with the flag of peace represents the other aspect of the ram. The qualities of true leadership include humility and submission to the cosmic law, as well as dynamism and power. A deep understanding and a constant consideration of the will of the Whole are also necessary. A ruler with these qualities is filled with a tremendous compassion which will allow him or her to sacrifice the self for the good of the whole.

The double eagles symbolize the inner and outer changes brought about by the creative energy of the Sun, and also refer to the Emperor's creative energy. He heralds the beginning of an enterprise, or a new phase in life. This new beginning may be an extension or expansion in the realm of rule, dominion, or mastery, or the conquering of new territories (also symbolized by the Emperor's legs, crossed in the form of the number 4; compare also the Prince of Wands). On the material plane, the new beginning may mean starting a promising new project, a change in career, travel or fatherhood. On the inner plane, new realizations may emerge. Insights in areas previously unfamiliar (discs to the right and left with exploding stars), or dramatic self-revelation and self-discovery, are also possible.

As long as the Emperor's powers are used for transformation and new beginnings, their effect is beneficial. But beware using them to preserve the status quo. When used to preserve the status quo, the structure of the Emperor's realm petrifies, his boldly determined expression becomes frozen. His authority, once grounded in wisdom, expresses as authoritarian domination. Living in fear of change, he attempts to nip any rebellion in the bud. He is then doomed. His own resistance to the flow of the Tao sooner or later will topple his reign.

Indication: *This is a propitious moment for a change or a new beginning. Trust your own energy and move with it.*

Questions: *What revitalization does your life need? Are there steps you would like to take toward this?*

Suggestion: *Examine yourself critically, especially in regard to your relations with subordinates and superiors.*

Affirmation: *I trust my power. I rule by serving, I serve by ruling.*

V THE HIEROPHANT

The Hierophant

Key Words: *Taurus; spiritual master, teacher, advisor, initiate, inner guide, spiritual father; highest transformation.*

This card is ruled by Taurus. The throne of the initiate is a bull surrounded by two elephants, whose nature is the same as that of the bull. The four cherubim, guardians of the altar, are found in the four corners of the picture: bull, lion, eagle, person; representing the different aspects of being. Taurus, the bull, is symbolic of Earth, matter, the physical. Leo, the lion, represents the element Fire, the capacity for intuition, willpower, and dynamism. The person represents the element Air (Aquarius), the mental-spiritual plane. The eagle represents the highest transformation, and is connected with the element Water (Scorpio), the realm of emotions.

The Hierophant has united all these elements in himself and has brought them to full expression. He is the Awakened One, the Fulfilled, the Enlightened. He is a true spiritual master, who acts as the intermediary between the human and the divine. He is the spirit made flesh (bull), or the final stage of human development in which the human is united with the godly.

The woman who stands before him holding the crescent moon and a sword is Venus, ruler of Taurus. She holds the symbols for wisdom and emotion, a sign that these are in balance. The Hierophant has united the female and male within himself, and evolved each fully.

When the male and female are united, the child Horus is born. He is naked, unprotected, vulnerable, full of openness and trust in Existence. He represents true wisdom, expressed in the natural innocence of a child. Anyone who spends time in the presence of the Hierophant is touched by this quality. All defense mechanisms must be dropped in order to come fully into contact with his Being.

His head is surrounded by five white rose petals, symbolic of love in its purest, most perfect form. This is the love which can see the other, and give what is really needed at that moment. It may not always be something the other wants or wishes. A true master does not fulfill the disciples' wishes. Truth is a provocation which can shake us out of the heavy sweet sleep of unconsciousness. Only those who are free of self-seeking motivation can wield the truth in this way, like Jesus whipping the money-lenders out of the temple.

The serpent of transformation at the top of the painting is touched by nine nails. They are reminiscent of the crown of thorns, a reminder of the pain and suffering with accompany every transformation. True transformation can happen only in an attitude of receptiveness (bull), sensitivity (dove), trust, and in surrender to divine love.

The dark background emphasizes the function of the Hierophant, who brings the light of Consciousness into the darkness of ignorance.

Indication: *The search for the Self leads you into spiritual realms. This card can point to a meeting with a spiritual teacher or master. Be open!*

Question: *Is there any master of wisdom (past or present) to whom you feel attracted?*

Suggestions: *Involve yourself with the teachings of spiritual masters. Seek the presence of a master or teacher. Involve yourself in groups for personal growth. Be honest, open and receptive in these groups. Pay attention to the instructions of your heart.*

Affirmation: *There is only one voice worth listening to, the voice of my own heart.*

VI THE LOVERS

Key Words: *Gemini; love, attraction, approaching, connection, union of opposites through Love; becoming conscious through relationship.*

The card shows the marriage of the Emperor and Empress. The ceremony is performed by the Hermit, one of the forms of the god Mercury. He is completely hidden by his robes to symbolize that the origin of all things lies beyond the reach of the manifest and the intellect.

The lovers represent two opposites which yearn for and are attracted to one another. This duality which is reflected in every aspect of existence, is existentially experienced in the relations between man and woman. Every attempt at approach, union, connection, is an expression of the passionate urge to re-establish this lost Oneness. Every individual, every man and every woman, contains the duality of male and female. These express themselves in different, often contradictory, personal characteristics.

Psychologists have recognized for a long time that each partner in a relationship mirrors the mental and spiritual condition of the other. Usually your partner mirrors aspects that are undeveloped and un-animated in yourself. What you feel you are missing in yourself you see in the other. This is an opportunity to have vitally important experiences on the way toward awareness. The lesson can't be grasped theoretically, through intellectual examination, or by wallowing in senti-ment. It demands direct, existential experiencing. It requires letting yourself in for all dimensions of joy, ecstasy, mutual enrichment, as well as the pain, struggle and annihilation necessary for growth. A relationship that is vital and alive allows those involved to experience all dualities, all opposites; with love comes jealousy, with harmony comes disharmony, with unity comes separation, with the excitement of becoming acquainted comes the sobering sense of estrangement.

If studying in this »school of life« can be said to have a goal, it is to become whole, total individuals. Only when you can find your oneness and inner harmony will you approach that goal of total self-unfolding. The bliss we all vainly seek outside ourselves is only to be found and developed in ourselves. Every disturbance that stirs us, every discontentment which simply leads us on to greater discontentment, acts to derail us on our search for real stillness and inner peace. This is the reason spiritual masters repeatedly say that an intelligent person quickly comes to the understanding that no relationship can be really satisfying, love leads us to an even greater understanding, but we cannot just be that love.

Back now to the symbols of the card. All symbols are presented in pairs, in readiness to meet the opposite. The transformation occurs in the union of the wedding. This is represented by the winged orphic egg and the snake coiled arround it. The children hold in their hands the symbols of the different planes to be affected by the transformation; body (club), intellect (spear), emotions (cup), and spirit (flowers). The lances which build a border in the background represent the conflict between limitation and freedom, connection and independence, com-ponents of every relationship.

There are three other symbols from the zodiac to be seen; Leo, Scorpio, Sagittarius. the lion (Leo) represents the male principle in nature, and indicates the creativity which may grow out of the union. The white eagle represents Scorpio, the scorpion in its transformed state. It mirrors the feminine component, the surrender to one's own emotional depths. Cupid, as Sagittarius, shows the need for direct, honest interchange.

Indications: *Drawing this card may inaicate a wonderful and exciting love relationship. Current relationships either deepen or end. New methods for personal growth and integration of your own opposing aspects present themselves as you turn toward and interact with a partner or group.*

Questions: *What do you seek in the people you love? What comprises a fulfilling relationship for you?*

Suggestion: *Play Tarot with your partner. Use the cards to learn more about your relationship. See instructions on page 185-186.*

Affirmation: *I am now ready to meet the partner I have always longed to meet.*

VII THE CHARIOT

Key Words: *Cancer; new beginning, change for the good; introspection, meditation, spiritual path.*

The driver sits in meditation posture in a chariot which has not yet begun to move. He is clothed in golden armor and is meditating on the Holy Grail which is rotating in his hands. The Grail symbolizes the Wheel of Fortune. The driver is examining all possible consequences before daring to set the chariot in motion on a new beginning, for once the driver has chosen to start, there is no turning back. Nothing will be able to arrest the journey.

This card refers generally to imminent new beginnings. It can point to a journey, or the start of some new phase (relationship, living situation, job) of life. Nothing should be decided precipitously. Everything requires exact examination and preparation. But once all the ground-work is done, the new start should not be put off unnecessarily. Everything points toward favorable developments.

The driver's armor is golden and set with ten crystals. It is a symbol of Cancer's protective shell, providing shelter and protection for the inner transformation (the color gold) and the development of clarity (crystals). In times of breakthrough or new beginnings you need the protection and support of a loving atmosphere which provides a sense of safety and security. The oncoming change brings with it much excitement and unrest. This is a time to avoid chaotic, disorganized, or loveless relationships.

The new start leaves behind the boring routine of daily life. Inspiration and ideas abound, and expand your areas of activity. This is symbolized by the concentric blue circles in the background. You are now in a position to engage successfully in many different activities. This variety of activity will enrich and stimulate you. Despite the bustle, your highest goal will not be forgotten. The road upon which the chariot stands is paved with golden stones. This is the regal path travelled by every spiritual seeker in search of self-knowledge and inner transformation.

The four sphinxes (bull, lion, person, eagle) are the energies which will set the chariot in motion. They have exchanged heads and bodies, and assist each other. Once the right direction is chosen, their energies will combine and be set in motion to assure successful progress. Your trust in your own powers and perceptions will grow.

Indication: *The oncoming change promises to lead to a positive phase of your life. Ready yourself, put your affairs in order, examine the possibilities. You will leave much behind.*

Questions: *What area of your life will be changing? Are you ready to ring out the old and ring in the new?*

Suggestion: *Seek or create for yourself a loving, secure environment. There you can plan the change or journey. Your body also needs attention and activity now.*

Affirmation: *I am putting my life in order and preparing for the new beginning.*

VIII ADJUSTMENT

Key Words: *Libra; balance, centering, equilibrium; balancing of opposites; justice.*

This card portrays the sign of Libra. It is a fascinating picture of balance. A young woman (the feminine aspect to The Fool), holds the great magic sword between her legs and balances on her toes. Looking carefully, you will see that she is actually balancing only on the tip of the sword. Only absolute concentration and stillness, which come from finding one's inner center, will allow this condition of equilibrium to take place. The slightest distracting thought will cause her to waver and destroy the balance she has found, the balance that is the nature of the Universe.

The predominant colors are blue and green. Blue is the color of spiritual and intellectual powers, such as thinking, ideas, wisdom; green is the color of creativity, the power to put ideas into action. The downward-pointing sword lends a similar meaning. The powers of thought are directed toward, and put into contact with, the earth, and serve her. (See also Ace of Swords.)

The woman's shoulders are covered by the ostrich feathers associated with MAAR, the Egyptian god of Justice. Her face is masked, all her attention is turned inward. This makes her receptive to ideas and direction from the inner guide.

She bears on her head the crown of Thoth, the Egyptian god of Wisdom. Hanging from the crown are the large bowls of the cosmic scales, Alpha and Omega, with which the universe weighs all.

This card is a summons to avoid all extremes in your daily life. This may refer to emotional disturbances in relationships, or at work, in some creative activity, or in dealing with money. Total centeredness and inner balance are needed if the great new ideas arising now are to bear fruit. From a position of balance everything develops in a balanced way: in its place, given its appropriate value.

The storms of life throw us out of balance again and again. The constant change between being centered and uncentered is the process which teaches us to be more conscious from moment to moment in order to retain that inner peace and clarity when we find it.

Indication: *Pay attention to what situations in your daily life tend to throw you off-balance. Discover the conditions under which you find harmony again. Carry this quality with you more and more as you move through your daily activities.*

Questions: *What helps you to reach your meditative center, and to stay there? What happens when you lose your center?*

Suggestions: *Take time regularly for some form of meditation which steadies you in your center. Breathe into the Hara center (a hand's width below the navel), and collect your energies there.*

Affirmation: *I am at rest in my own center.*

IX THE HERMIT

IX

The Hermit   ♍

Key Words: *Virgo; finding one's own light; going inward; completion, harvest; resting in one's own center; wise guide.*

The Hermit has set out in search of internal fulfillment and has found the light within. He is so fulfilled by the wealth of the inner realm that the external world appears colorless and unimportant. When you repose in yourself, you have come home. There is no reason to chase after the deceptive light of that which is external and transitory.

However, the journey inward also has its difficult and troublesome aspects. You need courage, and trust in yourself, in order to embark on this journey, for before you reach the sought-for light, you are led through the apparently danger-filled realms of your own shadow. These are represented on the card by the poisonous snake and the three-headed hell-hound, Cerberus. Two of Cerberus' heads look forward, one looks back. His attention is directed partly toward the past in order to make sure all important details have been brought to completion. All unfinished business must be attended to before the available energies can be applied to the new. The integration of the animal in us is also a prerequisite to the emergence of a whole, total Being.

The transforming light of inner clarity fills, bit by bit, all levels of his being. The sheaves ripen, the fruits of his surrender to the internal Self become visible. The grain can be harvested and shared with others. Whoever has found the inner reality can share the experience of transformation with other seekers.

The Hermit is not revered by others, and is rarely understood. He is an individual who hears a different drummer, not satisfied with the superficialities of the masses. The Hermit enters only into those relationships which offer union of deeper levels. If this is not possible, the Hermit prefers to remain alone.

This card admonishes you to heed your inner wisdom, and gather together with other people who will be supportive on the shared path. The goal of this path is to find the inner voice and learn to listen to it. Discover your inner guide and become well acquainted with your inner healer.

Indications: *Accept your aloneness! Don't concern yourself with people who don't understand you, who would rather see you be a part of the herd. If you should meet a wise leader or teacher, join her or him.*

Question: *Have you any unresolved situations or relationships in your life?*

Suggestion: *Make a list of all situations which you now wish to resolve or in some way bring to completion. Whoever embarks on the search for the internal light must not be encumbered by unresolved conflicts. Accounts must be settled.*

Affirmation: *I enjoy my aloneness. I can stop being alone whenever I wish.*

X FORTUNE

Key Words: *Jupiter; new beginning, expansion, creativity, big break-through; self-realization; unexpected fortune.*

In the midst of energy whirlwinds and lightning bolts turn the ten-spoked Wheel of Fortune. It is a symbol of wholeness, in constant motion yet unchanging in its completeness.

The three figures – sphinx, ape and crocodile – represent three Egyptian gods. The sphinx unifies the four magic virtues; knowledge, will, daring and silence. Wisdom arises through the unification of animal instincts and intuitive intellectual powers. The sword in the sphinx's paw testifies to incorruptible powers of discrimination and the ability to think clearly.

The ape on the left side of the wheel symbolizes flexibility (see the Magus). It looks as if he is the one who keeps the wheel in constant motion.

The crocodile represents the god of creativity (see The Fool). It holds two tools in its hands. In the right is the Egyptian Ankh, symbol of life; every creative act brings something to life. The staff with the hook at the end is a symbol of the possibility we have to forge our own luck. We can recognize and attract good opportunities and make use of them.

The center of the wheel represents the Sun, origin and unification of all creative energies. It is also a symbol of awareness, realization, enlightenment. In the Sun is the absolute center, the center of the cyclone which, despite the constant movement at the periphery, remains still and unchanged. This is the inner seed, the witness who remains untouched by the ups and downs of duality; joy and sadness, hope and fear.

But right now we are observing the periphery of the wheel. We are filled with joy by the breakthrough into clarity, the great fortune this very moment brings us. Life holds out unexpected gifts and possibilities to us. Now we need watchful eyes in order in order to perceive the gifts and possibilities offered to us.

Indications: *If no miracles are happening, something is wrong! You stand before the possibility of a great breakthrough! Use the moment!*

Questions: *Are you really ready for the great fortune? What's still standing in the way?*

Suggestion: *Write down, or list to a trusted person what Fortune means to you in your present situation. Then make a new list of everything which prevents your experiencing Fortune right now.*

Affirmation: *I am now ready for the miracle of my life.*

XI LUST

Key Words: *Leo; passion; multidimensional creativity, talents; strength; integration of animalistic energies; overcoming old fears and conditionings.*

The traditional name of this card is Strength. Crowley renamed the card because its meaning includes much more than the word »strength« expresses. Lust means more than vital strength, it includes also the joy in, and the enjoyment of, that strength; it means also passion. A woman sits on the back of a lion. In her right hand she holds the Holy Grail which is enflamed with the fire of love and death, and raises it into the heights.

The card is a representation of divine intoxication, divine ecstasy, divine madness. The woman appears intoxicated. The lion is also enflamed by lust. His seven heads are those of an angel, a saint, a poet, an adulteress, a daring man, a satyr, and a lion-serpent. They symbolize different aspects and viewpoints which now unite and meld together as a single perceptive force in one orgiastic experiencing. They are independant of morality and limiting rationalism. The energy forms expressed here are those of an archetypal creative Order.

The animal within is not tamed and integrated through struggle and repression, but through affirmation and surrender. The strength you gain in this process helps you overcome old fears and restrictive conditioning, represented by the folded hands and the faces of the saints seen dimly in the background.

The ten faintly radiating circles, scattered behind the woman and lion, show the fading old moral ideals which will now be replaced by the fresh ones pulsating at the top of the picture, symbolizing the new light which streams snake-like in all directions to destroy the world and create it anew. This process of recreation is again symbolized in the lion's tail, a serpent with a lion's head.

The woman's head is turned completely toward the urn of fire. She is totally absorbed in the energy of transformation inherent in any total and conscious surrender. This is the secret of Tantra, the awareness which perceives the fullness of each moment and accepts all of life, rejecting nothing.

Lust reveals its valuable creative potential only when fully tasted, savored and drunk in. Only then can it be understood and be implemented in your own process of becoming aware. The way to the light passes through all aspects of darkness.

Indication: *If you are ready to accept all which you find in yourself, you will be able to move through everything with deep sensitivity, awareness, love and understanding.*

Questions: *What areas of your life would you like to live out more fully? What has prevented you from doing so in the past? Are you ready to deal with this anew?*

Suggestion: *Take everything in with more awareness. We often experience emotions such as love, sadness, pain, rage or fear as obstacles only because we have never learned to use them as potential energy.*

Affirmation: *I enjoy living to the utmost.*

XII THE HANGED MAN

The Hanged Man

Key Words: *congealed; end of a situation or relationship which is stuck; letting go, giving up, surrendering; learning to see in a new way; the necessity of breaking through old behavior patterns.*

The Hanged Man is nailed upside-down, a position in which the personal will is broken. The situation is at a stalemate: there is no more room to move. Escape of any kind has become impossible. The serpents of transformation and wisdom lay coiled and sleeping.

The Hanged Man is nailed to the wood of his petrified attitudes and viewpoints. His eyes are closed: he is blind to all which does not fit into the closed system of his concepts. Every new idea, every new impulse, is ignored or resisted.

His head is shaved. The hair, symbol of spiritual perception, is removed. The Hanged Man has even lost trust in his own intuition. All his efforts seem unpromising and doomed to failure.

However, even in the midst of this hopelessness, wonders can occur! The point has come at which you can no longer avoid seeing naked realities. There is nothing left but to face up to them and let go. This form of capitulation, the giving up of willfulness and frozen ideologies leads to far-reaching transformation; breaking through rigid behavior patterns, clearing away old rubbish, full surrender to the higher Self, freedom from narrow-mindedness and dogma. One who bows willingly to the cosmic order of the Universe is able to become one with the flow of the Tao. »Not my will, but Thy Will be done; for Thy Will is also mine.« The great reward for the deep surrender to the Whole is a one hundred eighty degree turn. The world can be seen from a new perspective!

Indications: *It is now possible for you to recognize where you are stuck and which areas of your life are congealed rather than flowing. There is nothing to do. The mere act of perceiving your reality clearly makes transformation possible.*

Questions: *In what areas of your life are you stuck? Are you ready to recognize and let go of your petrified thought and behavior patterns?*

Suggestion: *Draw another card for that which awaits you when you surrender.*

Affirmation: *I let go and realize, follow and accept the will of the divine in my life which reveals itself to me step by step.*

XIII DEATH

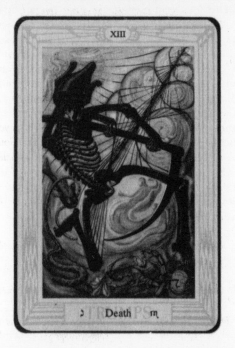

Key Words: *Scorpio; death and resurrection; transformation: scorpion, snake, eagle; becoming free of old ensnarements; external changes.*

As a rule, the card Death does not mean physical death. It generally points to radical external transformation. (The card XVI, The Tower, is the expression of internal change.)

Old relationships are demanding to be disintegrated. This process may be bound together with painful experiences. However, your drawing this card indicates your readiness. The act of letting go, difficult as it may be, will liberate you. Death shows two faces; one destroying and tearing down, the other freeing you from old bonds which have become confining, preventing Life. Which of these aspects will predominate depends on your attitude. Any desire to hold on or cling to old bonds will cause their death to appear that much more agonizing. Hesse tells us to let ourselves fall. When we have renounced our supports, even the earth under our feet; so that we listen to the guide in our hearts, then all is won. There is no more fear, no more danger, when we let go. *

The painting is dominated by the skeleton with its scythe ready to mow. It is poised in an extremely tense position, coiled, about to set into motion change, and transformation. The scorpion at the bottom of the picture holds its tail ready to sting. The blossoms of the water lily and the holy lily lay dying in the mud from which they at one time grew.

The next stage: the snake, symbol of transformation. It is prepared to deliver the deadly bite when appropriate. The fish, the old past, could become its victim. The phoenix can only rise after the fire of transformation has consumed all, turning it to ashes.

The skeleton is wearing the funeral head-covering used in ancient Egypt. This is a reference to the nessecity of carrying old ideas and concepts to their grave now, and burying them. Cords and bonds must be cut, imprisoned souls liberated from their bonds. The eagle, the final stage of transformation, unfolds its wings and rises.

Indications: *You are now ready to make the necessary changes in your life. Accept the pain that may come with the loss of the old.*

Question: *To what outdated relationships or situations are you clinging?*

Suggestion: *»Die before you die.« This traditional Sufi saying admonishes us to learn the art of dying. As long as any fear of death or letting go completely remains, we cannot live life fully. All clinging, every »no« prevents us from being in the natural flow of Life.*

Affirmation: *I now say: Yes to Death, Yes to myself.*

---

* Hermann Hesse, *Klein und Wagner*
  Published in USA (in compilation)
  by Farrar, Straus & Giroux, Inc., 19, Union Square West, New York, N.Y. 10003.
  Published in Great Britain
  by Jonathan Cape Ltd., 30 Bedford Square, London WC1 B3EL

XIV ART

Key Words: *Sagittarius; unification of opposites, balance; inner change, transformation, alchemy, a quantum leap; creative power.*

The alchemical union of fire and water portrayed above the head of the Fool, has now moved to the center of the picture. The whole card is characterized by symbols of integration, the unification of opposites.

The binding together of fire and water, light and dark, male and female, death and rebirth, is an internal process. The melting of contradictions is a major step toward oneness. The opposing forces transform themselves into a new state of being. The marriage of Emperor and Empress shown on the card The Lovers, reaches now its fulfillment. This is the highest art of transformation.

The bringing together of opposites is a preparation for generating something new. The large sun and the moons crossing it give birth to the stars in the background.

The dress is the color of creativity – green. The Latin sentence inscribed on the sun translates to »Examine the inner realms of the

Earth; by cleansing you will find the hidden stone.« This has many meanings on different levels (as do many of the images and symbols in this Tarot), but the most useful is seen in the context of the green dress (creativity) und suggests the necessity of bringing creative forces into contact with earth energy.

The lion and eagle, assistants in the alchemical process, have already completed their transformation. We saw them first on the card called The Lovers. They have grown in size and significance. The lion, representative of the element fire has taken on the color of water. The eagle, a higher form of the scorpion, and a representative of the element water, has taken on the color of fire. This image of balance, inversion and integration is repeated on the golden alchemical urn; the raven on the skull is a symbol of death and rebirth. The dark-skinned king now has a light-skinned face, and the light-skinned queen now has a dark-skinned face. The face of the queen, on the left, looks to the hand at the right, while the face on the right concentrates on the hand to the left. Water and fire pour into the urn. The fire consumes the water and the water extinguishes the fire.

The steam, energy of the new, rises. The arrow (in the center of the body) re-emphasizes this. The steam forms two rainbows, symbols of wholeness, which surrounds the shoulders of the androgynous figure. The eight circles on the chest (two are covered) symbolize symmetry and balance. The honeybees (on the Queen's robe on the card The Lovers) and the snakes (on the King's) have intermingled. The bees stand for art, perception and integration.

Indication: *The card Art is a challenge to look inward. In this phase of integrating opposites, the transformation process will not tolerate any further impulses or pushes from outside. To find the hidden stone, the diamond, you must look within.*

Question: *What does it mean now for you to find your »hidden diamond«?*

Suggestion: *Close your eyes and visualize a fountain of energy in your body. Bathe a while in this rejuvenating current.*

Affirmation: *I surrender to the transforming powers of the divine. I am an open channel for creative energy.*

XV THE DEVIL

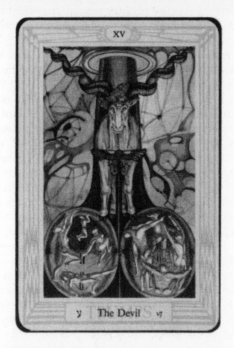

Key Words: *Capricorn; procreative energy, new vitality; humor; sensuality; sexuality; creative energy; individuality.*

The Devil is another of the cards which are most often misunderstood. To understand this card you have to free yourself of all popular moral and superstitious ideas.

The Devil is represented by the god Pan, in the form of a white mountain-goat with powerful twisted horns. The column behind him symbolizes the erect penis, the two globes below symbolize the testicles. This is a representation of creative energy in its most material and male aspect.

In the globes, like sperm cells, are four female and four male bodies, which are bringers of the new. The tremendous powers of generation are also symbolized by the staff with a winged globe and two snakes, the snakes of Horus and Osiris.

The phallic column reaches the upper edge of the painting. It reaches through the heavens, symbolized by the ring of the body of the star-goddess Nuith. The column also reaches downward deep into the center of the earth.

This connecting of earth's center and the cosmos is a wonderful image of creative union. This anchoring deep in the earth permits the dark brown earth energy to rise in order to melt with the golden yellow cosmic energy from above. This melting together of cosmic and earth energy inspires you in creative directions and makes you capable of manifesting this inspiration.

On Pan's forehead we see his open third eye. This indicates his extensive abilities in the realm of extra-sensory perception. He is a seer who can see not only the obvious, but also the deeper essence of what he observes.

His expression is one of very humorous satisfaction. All people who see the essence of the world can be recognized by their marked sense of humor (e.g., Castaneda's Don Juan). Only ignorant people are deadly serious, and are fully identified with their thoughts and actions. This imprisonment in the animal-material is the essence of our common conception of the devil. But Pan grins over people and their projections, with which they »demonize« him. In his wisdom he sees that, in fact, every desire, every imprisonment, all-possessiveness leads only to frustration and suffering. Human beings will only arrive at this insight through repeated direct experience. The more you learn to see or become aware, the more you can truly enjoy. When you are freed from all moralistic limitations you will surrender with utter sensuality to the enjoyment of the earth, discovering the ecstasy in every manifestation, tasting the divine in everything. You will enjoy and continue on, without clinging.

Indications: *There may be people who »demonize« you, make you out to be the devil. Meet them with humor and lightness. Accept what Life gives you. Keep your feet on the ground!*

Question: *Do you have some wish or desire you don't admit to?*

Suggestions: *Sit down comfortably to meditate. Pay attention to your breathing. Imagine that with every out-breath a root grows from the base of your spine deep into the center of the Earth; it will happen quickly. Now feel that with every in-breath Earth energy flows into you. It fills your entire body. Then let your awareness go to the crown of your head. Open yourself for the yellow-gold cosmic energy. Feel it mix with the Earth energy and fill your body.*

Affirmation: *I am the master of my life.*

XVI THE TOWER

Key Words: *Mars; far-reaching inner transformation; healing; the old is destroyed to make room for the new; spiritual renewal; self-knowledge.*

The power of the consuming, purifying fire destroys the old and sweeps it away. Nothing is spared; the tower of the ego will be shaken to its very foundations.

Anything you attempt to cling to will be destroyed by this transforming power. The apparent securities of the past have begun to waver and topple. All that remains is trust; the knowledge that all events in life arise from the endless love of the universe and bring us the possibility for learning and recognition. This understanding of the true nature of events transforms even apparent losses or painful disappointments into the valuable gifts they really are. Times of desperation and inner tension, when recognized, can become the most fruitful growing phases of our lives.

The Tower is also one of the highest cards for healing. Just as the extraction of a rotten tooth provides relief for the entire body, the destruction of stagnant situations and relations which hinder growth begins a healing process for your entire organism. Having a tooth extracted can be painful, but when the tooth is poisoning your system, there is no other choice. The strokes of fate may seem equally tragic and unfathomable, but they come to us only because we need them and have created them for ourselves either consciously or unconsciously. If you can recognize and accept these laws of the universe, you possess all you need for true liberation and total transformation to occur.

The eye of Horus illustrates awakened consciousness, which sees reality as it truly is. The dove with the olive branch symbolizes the compassion toward oneself and others which arises out of self-knowledge. It also symbolizes that which remains pure and whole throughout; the essence of being, from which all is created anew (the snake).

Indications: *You are in the midst of (or are about to enter into) an extremely intensive transformatory process. Whatever is destroyed or shaken within you serves to purify you and make room for for something new. Allow it!*

Question: *Are you ready to view yourself and Life with new eyes?*

Suggestion: *Observe yourself in daily life. Situations may seem to repeat themselves, but you will not continue to repeat old, limited, restrictive behavior patterns.*

Affirmation: *Everything that happens in my life is for the best.*

XVII THE STAR

Key Words: *Aquarius; inspiration, crystallization, self-recognition, radiating, clear vision, trust in the self; connection to universal intelligence.*

This card represents a beautiful process. Cosmic inspiration of the highest nature is received and made manifest on the material plane. The card is ruled by Aquarius. The medium, or water carrier in this process, is represented by the star goddes Nuith (see also XX The Aeon). She is fully open to the input from the spiritual plane, and passes it on in full service to the highest good. She is the channel used by divine energy to manifest on earth. In each hand she holds a cup through which the spiral vortices of energy pour. Her hair acts as an antenna to extend perception and flows to the earth, carrying with it the inspiration of the cosmic.

A new, crystal-clear vision lends form and purpose to that which a moment ago was only a vague impression. You gain a more penetrating view into the boundless potential of your development. The power of the inspiration you receive gives wings to your soul and lets the apparently impossible become manifest in marvelous ways.

A person led by this wisdom exudes such a quality of being, such a radiation, that other people are drawn as if by a magnet. The sheer force of spiritual transformation causes the masks of personality and the limitations of the small »I« to become meaningless. Stubborn will-fullness and fear can be dropped as the water-bearer gives herself up, more and more, to the workings of the newly-freed spirit.

The receptive antennas must, however, be subjected regularly to careful purifying and cleansing. If reception is disturbed by self-seeking tendencies, the tremendous energies at hand can have a devastating effect. Enthusiasm may become fanatacism, inspiration may become illusion. The emotions need to be watchfully observed. Just as the water flows from the cup of Nuith and turns to crystals, so must the emotions become crystalized. This means they must be clearly and definitely grasped. This cannot happen if you repress and control emotions, but only if you allow emotional unfolding to take place (symbolized by the rose blossoms). The butterflies, symbols of trans-formation, indicate that your own view of things will change and become liberated from the bonds of old conditioning.

Indications: *Let your star rise, and stay in contact with the earth. Trust your environment and find ways to let others share in it. You will be tested and recognized by the fruits you bear.*

Question: *Are you totally fulfilled in your present area of work?*

Suggestion: *Check to see if you are doing everything possible to bring your ideas to fruition.*

Affirmation: *My creative powers of imagination and my connection to all-encompassing consciousness show me the way to realize my ideas.*

XVIII THE MOON

Key Words: *Pisces; final testing; wrong turns, illusion; burning off karma; interaction or struggle with the subconscious; threshold to new levels of consciousness.*

The moon here is the waning moon. It is in the process of diving further and deeper into the darker realms of the soul. It is the time of final, and often most difficult, testing. The danger of forgetting your true goal in the darkness is very great. Temptations and illusory perceptions lurk along the way ready to lead you down the garden path! Be careful!

The upper part of the card shows a narrow passageway guarded by sinister sentries whose heads are those of wolves (Anubis, Egyptian god of Death). Behind them rise dark, threatening towers, symbols of the sentries' power. The guards hold the scepter of the Phoenix in one hand and the symbols for Mercury and Pluto as keys in the other. Jackals lurk at their feet ready to fall upon and devour the corpses of those who risk passing between the towers in uncertainty or out of mere curiosity.

The guarded entranceway is also a representation of the female sexual and birth organ, the vagina. The moon symbolizes here the unconscious aspect of the feminine; changeable, moist, shadowy, seductive, possessing an eery attraction. Everything appears mysterious, doubtful and bewitching.

But only by passing through this gateway will new life arise. The path to awareness leads us through unawareness, the unknown the menacing. Anyone who wishes to be a person of wisdom must first deal directly and fully with these areas of ignorance. Only through direct experience will you get to know them; the veils of illusion yield finally to the light as you recognize them for what they are. As the veils part, you gain valuable insight into the true mysteries hidden behind them.

An analogy to this process is the rite of initiation performed in many tribes. The introduction into the status of adulthood requires the completion of a very difficult and dangerous task for which long and careful preparation is needed.

The person who dares to pass through the portals needs unconquerable courage and the willingness to make the necessary preparations. Happy the one who has the good fortune to find a guide who can be trusted on this stage of the path! Yet even or perhaps especially in this case, tremendous awareness is required. All too many guides offer themselves with tempting promises without knowing the way themselves. Only by keeping in constant touch with the voice of your heart will you be able to turn mistakes into opportunities for progress in the path. When you truly follow the teachings of the heart, you will see that even a false path may have been a necessary learning step on the way.

The threshold to Death is also the threshold to a new life. This is the entry way into a higher consciousness. This is symbolized on the card by the sacred Egyptian beetle holding in its pincers the symbol for the sun. The beetle carries the renewing light into the darkness. Wherever this light of consciousness appears, the darkness disappears. In fact, the darkness is revealed as having been an illusion, mere shadows which appeared to exist only because something was blocking the flow of light. Getting to know what things are blocking the light for you and sweeping them aside are the first steps in transformation.

Indications: *You have heard the call of the unknown. You are on the threshold of new experience. Pay attention now to the voice of your heart, and scrutinize calmly and carefully the offers of assistance and guidance you may receive.*

Questions: *What inner regions feel strange, alien, unknown to you? Where are your blind spots? What experiences are you most afraid of?*

Suggestions: *Meditate regularly! Choose a technique you feel comfortable with and practice it daily for at least three months. Pay attention to the quality of your thoughts and images and write them down occasionally, or paint or draw them. Pay attention also to your nightly dreams.*

Affirmation: *It's always darkest just before the dawn.*

XIX THE SUN

Key Words: *Sun; highly creative energy; awareness; fulfilled love relationship; wisdom, spirituality; transformation.*

The sun radiates as the center, in the middle of the twelve astrological signs, and bathes everything in its light. From its interior blooms the rose of realization. Its light is the essence of clarity and highest consciousness and awareness.

Two children with butterfly wings dance on the green mountain of creativity. This is a symbol of a liberated partnership between man and woman. The freedom gained is expressed in ecstatic joy and enthusiasm. Now all energies are fully available for a common creative process. The energies will no longer be wasted in struggles over dominance, jealousy or boundaries.

The wings of their combined creativity, the experience of union in the service of the great Light, carry them aloft. They experience and enjoy fulfillment in every moment. There is no wished-for goal off in the future. Everything is here, and it is good.

The wall surrounding the tip of the mountain means that the highest peak of freedom and consciousness remains locked to these two. In order to pass beyond, they must leap one last special hurdle. The small entrance to the peak must be found by each of us.

In this state of ecstasy, a far-reaching alchemical transformation can take place. The person represented by the Moon is a reflector of light, while the person represented by the Sun has become a source of light, embodying the qualities of wisdom and spirituality. S/He is no longer just a mirror, like the Moon which reflects the Sun's light without being able to radiate light or warmth itself. S/He has found the ultimate source of inner light. S/He radiates divine wisdom and love upon the whole world, infusing it with the light of transformation.

Something new and transformational is being ripened in all of humankind, just as fruit is ripened through a chemical process caused by the Sun's warm rays. The birth of a »New Humanity« requires the completion of a process described in the old alchemical texts. The Phoenix burns, only to arise from the ashes a new, magnificent bird, and fly into the open sky. The light of consciousness will permeate all aspects of our being.

Indications: *The fulfillment of your wishes is possible here and now. Relax, and give yourself up to the dance. The right partners will find each other.*

Question: *What task or project is on the agenda for you now?*

Suggestions: *Visualize the light and warmth of the Sun in your chest and heart. For the next few days, remind yourself several times daily that the sun is shining in and through you.*

Affirmation: *I am in harmony with the divine Light which fills and guides me.*

XX THE AEON

Key Words: *highly discriminating or discerning; open to criticism; critical self-analysis.*

The central part of the card is enveloped by the stylized body of the star-goddes Nuith. She spreads night over the heavens in order to provide a background for the stars. During the day, she is once again swallowed up by the sun. Her companion is Hadit, represented by a winged ball of fire. He represents the omniscient view, the view from all sides at once. The union of these two creates the child Horus. He is a double god, possessing both a passive and an active form.

The eye of Horus sees the totality. He can see what has fallen out of harmony. His clear insight serves as a basis for an all-encompassing critical power of discrimination. Criticism based on such deep perception can be communicated in a manner that motivates and inspires, rather than condemns others. Discernment which springs from real insight is constructive and free of dogma.

The Aeon points to a need for well-thought-out judgement of the situation. A long, difficult work process may be required before you finally reach this judgement.

All-encompassing insight cannot be achieved solely through the intellect. Body, Spirit and Soul (the three figures at the bottom of the picture) are drawn into the process of forming a judgement, and during this process you will instinctively move toward that which will support your blossoming, and move away from that which will offer no help.

The god of Wisdom (Ohyros), shown as a winged serpent at the top of the painting, is a symbol of the vast powers of thought available to the mind which reflects reality directly, freed from the ballast of prejudice or preconceptions. Judgement arises from direct personal experience. Finally, it is life itself, and no longer the limited individual consciousness, which becomes the source of all judgement.

Indications: *You are being challenged to drop your »worm's eye view,« to see things from a higher plane. When you have recognized greater timespans (aeons) and other contexts (which you are increasingly ready to do), you will then tend more and more to observe things in their being-ness: to see free from evaluations:*

Suggestion: *Meditate on the following statement: One sign of ignorance is indicated by some belief in injustice and unhappiness.*

Question: *Which methods will you use to gain deeper insight and greater wisdom?*

Affirmation: *God is the Unknown, the mysterious. The more I know that I don't know, the closer I am to the Divine.*

XXI THE UNIVERSE

Key Words: *Saturn; completion, cosmic union; travel liberation from bondage; burning off karma.*

This is the last card of the Major Arcana. It closes the circle which began with The Fool. The great task has been brought to completion, and returns to the innocence and ingenuousness of The Fool. The drop disappears into the ocean, and the ocean pours into the drop. This completion is, at the same time, a new beginning on a higher level of being. The final goal is reached – the return to the original cosmic Oneness.

Now you see yourself and the world as it really is (Eye of Horus in the upper right). All garments and masks have become superfluous and useless because you are at one with your original nature. You are whirling, caught up in the perpetual dancing motion of the universe. The boundaries of your small »I« dissolve in orgasmic union with the universe.

The nude woman dances the dance of liberation. Through the Eye of Horus she has seen into the nature of limitations. With this insight (symbolized by the sickle she still holds in her right hand), she cuts through the web of ensnarement. Even the gigantic serpent of transformation has lost its function. The energy has been transformed and a new quality exists. The serpent has outlived its usefulness; there is nothing left which its poisonous bite could destroy.

The four cherubim blow the all-pervading spirit in all four directions. »See, all is new!«*

Indication: *It is now possible for you to see things as they really are. The stage is set for a new beginning or a favorable completion. The events in your life are in harmony with the universe.*

Questions: *From what aspects of your life is it time to free yourself? Is there a journey or an enterprise waiting for you to set it in motion?*

Suggestions: *Trust your perceptions! Make a list of all unfinished situations whose resolution would give you a sense of relief.*

Affirmation: *I am one with the universe.*

---

* *The New Testament*, Revelations of St. John, Apocalypse I, 1–8

THE
COURT CARDS

KNIGHT OF WANDS

Knight of Wands

Key Words: *the fiery aspect of fire; dynamic forward motion; increased insight; coming changes.*

The Knight of Wands symbolizes the mastery of growth and inner development. In his left hand is the burning torch (see Ace of Wands) with which he burns away all negativity which stands in his way. He has taken on the task of removing all abstacles and blocks on the path towards his own growth.

His flowing cape is made of flame. His helmet is ornamented with a unicorn's head whose horn symbolizes the third eye. His own vision has become a vehicle (horse) for decisive dealing with the outer world.

As a reptile grows, it must, from time to time, crawl out of the old skin which has become too tight. The knight's armor, made of reptile skin, symbolizes dropping all that is old and narrow, and leaping forward courageously.

The energy created by increased perception is set free and now manifests; it is unstoppable. Even difficult situations will move in a constructive direction.

Indications: *Be awake, ready for people or situations which could produce dynamic changes in your consciousness. Be grateful for this gift from existence. Receive it, and don't cling to it.*

Questions: *Does your present situation allow your energies to develop and unfold fully? If not, what must be removed or changed?*

Suggestion: *Seek out situations and opportunities that challenged you! Engage withh all your energy.*

Affirmation: *Every challenge which arises helps me grow. Every storm strengthens my roots.*

QUEEN OF WANDS

Queen of Wands

Key Words: *the watery aspect of fire; self-knowledge, change, compassion.*

The Queen of Wands has mastered self-knowledge. She has looked deep into her own nature which has led to a transformation of her being.

The story says that she at one time had black hair, and the panther, her companion, had black fur. The transformation she underwent left her with golden blond hair, and turned the panther into a lion. However, her knowledge of her former condition filled her with compassion for those creatures not yet freed. In order to be able to help others, she chooses to wear reddish-brown hair, and keeps the lion in the form of a leopard, whose black spots bear witness to the darkness of the past.

The queen sits in a fiery throne wearing an armor of scales with a fish emblem on the breast. It is the unifying of water and fire, of intuitive recognition and emotional involvement, which effect inner transformation. Her crown of intellectual clarity and expanded perception still bears the nails of the crown of thorns, a reminder of the humiliation and suffering which preceded her transformation. Her eyes are closed in quiet ecstasy. The consciousness is turned inward and her presence radiates the blessedness of inner peace. The pine cone at the end of the wand symbolizes spiritual growth. The wand held in this position reminds us to ground our self-realization in the earth, as well as to allow others to share in it.

Indication: *You have worked on yourself and made progress. It's time to learn how to share this with others. Let your self-realization be expressed in your daily life!*

Questions: *How can you share what you have found for yourself with other people?*

Suggestion: *Meditate on the following statement: »Learning is finding out what you already know. Action is showing that you know. Teaching is letting others know that they know it as well as you.«**

Affirmation: *I am a radiant being filled with light and love.*

---

* Richard Bach, *Illusions, the Adventures of a Reluctant Messiah;* Delacorte Press / Eleanore Friede, N.Y., N.Y.

PRINCE OF WANDS

Prince of Wands

Key Words: *the airy aspect of fire; intensity; blossoming love; intuitive creativity; out of the darkness, into the light.*

The Prince sits with his arms outspread, as his fiery chariot moves forward swiftly. A few dark marks in the background hint at the darkness which he is now leaving behind. The general impression he makes is one of definiteness, openness, and freedom. He is naked, meaning he does not need to hide or protect himself. He holds a Phoenix-scepter in his right hand, a symbol of power and energy. He conquers new areas of his life like a pioneer (his legs form the number four, as on IV, The Emperor). His heart opens and he sees the world with new eyes.

The Prince of Wands personifies the mastery of intuitive creativity (the green color in the flames). All senses are geared toward being used for creative purpose. He trusts in his intuition, and surprises others with his original ideas and solutions. Nothing can hinder or limit this creative flow. The blazing fire in the chariot keeps him in motion.

By surrendering to love (lotus blossoms at his heart) he rises above himself. Wings of Phoenix feathers lift him and allow him to view the world from an elevated perspective.

The Prince of Wands is a fascinating expression of youthful, bubbling-over energy, and joy of life. His thoughts are daring and filled with creative power (winged lion above him). His trust in his perception frees him, allowing him to move beyond former limitations in thought and action.

The Prince of Wands is perfectly ready to engage himself fully in facing life's tests and challenges, but his greatest lesson is that his strong will can only help him toward his goal when it is in harmony with the will of the Whole.

Indications: *You have all you need! Don't let yourself be contained! Don't let yourself be slowed down! Life is prepared to receive you. Trust your boundless creative potential!*

Question: *What challenges are present now in your life?*

Suggestion: *Spread your arms wide and breathe deeply into your heart.*

Affirmation: *I love life and life loves me.*

PRINCESS OF WANDS

Princess of Wands

Key Words: *the earthy aspect of fire; being freed from fear; new beginning; optimism; increased perception.*

The fear is conquered! The Princess of Wands, naked, open, un-protected, has vanquished the tiger of fear (see The Fool). Her staff bears the symbol of the Sun. The feathers on her head indicate her increased perception and sense of justice which she has gained by overcoming her fear.

She dances her ecstatic dance in a huge flame. Beside her, on an altar ornamented with rams' heads, the fire of Spring, new beginnings, burns high. The fiery-red background symbolizes passion, vitality, and flaming energy. When fear disappears, undreamed-of springs of enthusiasm and joy bubble up, revitalizing our lives. Our self-limiting fears, the tiger's corpse, can be buried and forgotten.

Indications: *Your old fears have lost their power over you. Their dead remains cannot frighten you any longer. Reflect now on your greatest strengths.*

Question: *What's the next step in your life? Find it fearlessly!*

Suggestion: *Learn about ways of transforming fearful feelings. Get involved, for example, in dance, trance work or ecstatic forms of meditation.*

Affirmation: *My greatest strength is... As I accept my fear, it is transformed into love.*

KNIGHT OF CUPS

Knight of Cups

Key Words: *the fiery aspect of water; surrender to beloved ones; capacity for giving; reaching higher emotional planes; spiritual relationships.*

The Knight of Cups has large wings with which he soars on his powerful white horse. He wears green armor, and the cup in his outstretched right hand contains Cancer, the Crab. The water sign Cancer can refer to familial relationships. But here the idea of family must be enlarged to include also any chosen relationships, especially those with spiritual connections (or spiritual communities).

The pale blue wings of the spirit uplift emotional relationships to higher levels of exchange and mutual understanding. The peacock, symbol of vanity, has also been uplifted. He unfolds his beauty and offers it, without haughtiness, to the service of the higher.

The green armor represents the Knight's highly creative ability to give expression to his deep emotions. The gifts he gives are expressions of his striving toward more and more perfect forms of emotional interchange.

Indication: *You yearn for intensive interchange with those of like mind and like outlook.*

Question: *How can the interchange in your relationships be enriched?*

Suggestion: *Seek your true family, the community in which you feel at home. There you will find the quality of communication you long for.*

Affirmation: *I am finding the contact I now need.*

QUEEN OF CUPS

Queen of Cups

Key Words: *the watery aspect of water; as above, so below; emotions shown openly; motherhood; emotional integrity.*

The Queen's form is enclosed in light-beams, so you only see her if you look closely. Her being cannot be understood intellectually. You must feel and sense it. She is shrouded in mystery and if you wish to comprehend this mystery, you will have to go deeply into the realm of sensitivity and feeling.

The calm sea on which she rests mirrors her image almost perfectly. What she radiates outwardly is reflected in (or is a reflection of) the deepest emotional reaches of her being. She is in contact with her feelings and shows them openly and authentically. The people around her may not always understand her, but that is not a problem for her. She will not compromise emotionally, for in order to do so, she would have to deny herself, and might lose the glow of her beauty in doing so.

The white lotus blossoms on the lake, and in her hand, symbolize love of a giving nature. Lotus roots come out of the dark, muddy depths of the water, but the leaves and petals of the lotus remain untouched by the mud and water. Water rolls off the petals, or rests on them as beads of water. They remain connected to the water and mud, growing from them, but are different and separate. Blossoming love, too, grows from unconscious realms of instinct and drive, and is fed by it. The light of consciousness causes unconscious energies to arise in new form. The old appears in a new light, is transfigured, and emotional rebirth has taken place.

The stork, messenger of the returning spring, is harbinger of the new. This card can be seen as having some connection with motherhood (see also Princess of Disks and The Empress). The lotus in the Queen's hand is also the lotus of Isis, the Great Mother. Cancer, the Crab, in the shell-shaped cup also indicates the domestic realm of the family.

Indication: *By showing your feelings openly you become beautiful. There may be people who don't understand you; don't concern yourself about it! There are enough others with whom you can share your feelings.*

Question: *Are you open to your emotions and feelings?*

Suggestion: *Trust your feelings! Live in harmony with them!*

Affirmation: *My openness and vitality makes me beautiful.*

PRINCE OF CUPS

Prince of Cups

Key Words: *the airy aspect of water; desires, wishes, craving; possibility for transformation.*

The central task of the Prince of Cups is to master dealing with emotional needs. Air, in the context of water, symbolizes strong passions, as does the astrological sign Scorpio. The Prince's coach, reminiscent of a seashell, is drawn by a scorpion/eagle. This can be seen as an allusion to the possibility of transformation. The coach drives over the water of emotions but never touches it.

Wishes and desires must be perceived and recognized. They are fundamental driving force in our lives. It is only possible to use and master them if you are wide awake and alert. Instead of supressing them, you can use them in the process of becoming more aware. When seen this way, they are a vehicle that hepls us journey into the world within.

The snake, symbol of change and wisdom, awakens and rises up. The eagle on the Prince's helmet hints at the possibilities of spiritual liberation. The realization of these possibilities is a task which still lies before him. All too engrossed in looking at the snake, he forgets the lotus blossom (love) which now points downward. As he learns to integrate the driving forces of desire, the lotus will be able to develop and grow upright again.

Indications: *Accept your sexual needs and passions and live them out with awareness. You will discover a lot in this process. Give yourself totally to the experience, and observe yourself in it.*

Question: *What secret wishes are you unwilling to admit to?*
Suggestion: *Spend some time each day visualizing yourself your desires without getting lost in them.*

Affirmation: *I now live out my sexual desires. This makes me more vital and fulfilled.*

PRINCESS OF CUPS

Princess of Cups

Key Words: *the earth aspect of water; emotional freedom; jealousy conquered; trust in the self.*

The Princess of Cups is represented as a dancing figure. She is free, not imprisoned by emotions; for a swan, rising above her head, shows the independence and freedom she has gained. She has cast off the bonds of possessiveness and manipulation. Freed from jealousy, she is surrounded by grace, kindness and clarity (indicated by the crystals on her gown).

With great tenderness and gentleness she holds the cup with the turtle in her hand as a hint of the protection she lovingly assures herself and others. The white lotus flower in her outstretched left hand represents her readiness to be a giving lover. The outstretched arm symbolizes the distance she has taken from herself which makes it possible for her love to unfold in its purest form. The dolphin's eyes are crystals, meaning that the past can now be seen with clarity and can be brought to completion.

Indications: *Trust your feelings and perceptions. You are on the right path.*

Question: *Is there anything else preventing you from being fully free? You now have the opportunity to let go of it as well.*

Suggestion: *Imagine you are surrounded by water and are dancing the dance of salvation and freedom with light, flowing movements.*

Affirmation: *The more I love myself, the more I can share with others.*

KNIGHT OF SWORDS

Knight of Swords

Key Words: *the fiery aspect of air; goal-oriented, ambition, flexible intellectual powers; passion, vehemence.*

The Knight of Swords in his gold-green armor goes hunting, riding at full gallop, the embodiment of his goal-oriented mental activity. He knows where he is bound, and will not rest until he arrives at his destination. He has remarkable powers of concentration. Thoughts and ideas come to him with lightning speed; he is a master of imaginative and flexible thinking, which he uses to achieve his goals (gold-green armor). The four propellers refer to the four heavenly directions and indicate that the power of thought is bounded neither by time nor space.

His strong intellectual determination is unified with a deep emotional perceptiveness. Only goals which are emotionally charged can kindle such passion. Body, intellect and spirit (the three swallows) are in harmony and fly alongside him.

Both swords, the long one in his right hand, and the short one in his left, will be employed equally. They represent two potential energies, *yang* (male, analytical) and *yin* (feminine, intuitive) which will be needed in the proper balance in order for him to advance. He appears to be one with his galloping horse, because of his well balanced and correctly applied abilities.

Indication: *You are in a good position now to forge plans, set goals and bring them to fruition.*

Questions: *Do you know your goal? What happens once you achieve it?*

Suggestion: *Imagine how you will best be able to enjoy your success.*

Affirmation: *I know my goal and I know what I am working towards. Each goal is just a milestone on the way to my ultimate destination.*

QUEEN OF SWORDS

Queen of Swords

Key Words: *the watery aspect of air; cutting through old masks and roles; clarity; rational, intellectual, logical, objective.*

Setting aside your masks, renouncing the security offered by playing familiar roles means the voluntary giving-up of habitual defense mechanisms. By using the sword of penetrating insight you come to recognize that the masks you wear not only protect and camouflage, but also separate you from your Self and others. Energetic cutting through of your masks liberates you and the Queen of Sword leads you out of the surrounding clouds into clarity and openness.

The crystals behind her head, symbols of new clarity, support the head of a child. Behind the discarded masks are revealed a natural, child-like innocence that is now set free. The openness and receptiveness of a child, in conjunction with sharp, crystal clear insight into a person or a situation is a basic requirement for the work of a counselor or therapist. S/He must be prepared to let the masks drop, and may not allow her/himself to become entangled in the emotional complexities of a situation. Only in this way does the counselor earn real trust, or retain a real capability to offer healing in a helpful environment.

Indications: *You are in the process of separating yourself more and more from old roles and behavior patterns. This may bring painful experiences with it. But it's worth it! The clarity you gain frees you.*

Questions: *Which are the roles you most easily and most often hide behind? Are you ready to drop them?*

Suggestion: *Observe yourself in your different roles. Some you will continue to play, but now with more awareness. You will play them until you no longer identify yourself with them.*

Affirmation: *My only duty in life is to remain true to myself.*

PRINCE OF SWORDS

Prince of Swords

Key Words: *the airy aspect of air; intuition, creative thinking; cutting through all entanglements; becoming free of limited ideas and models; clear perception.*

The Prince of Swords wears tight, webbed, green armor. He is a master of creative ideas, thinking and planning. A prerequisite for being able to think creatively is unrestricted freedom. The creative thought process cannot tolerate being limited in any way. This is why the Prince swings his arm so far back to cut the connection with the figures pulling the wagon with full force. These figures are symbols of confining ideas and feelings, or limiting relationships, which might slow the chariot's progress.

The crystal in the chariot is shaped like a double pyramid. It shows perception becoming crystallized. This is a good time to give shape and form to ideas.

Sometimes problems appear insurmountable to us because of old, limiting belief systems and convictions, for example, »I am weak and dependent,« or, »If I assert myself, I will be punished«, or, »I am basically clumsy.« In some past situation, perhaps in our childhood, such feelings may have had a certain validity, but now they have no relation to our present reality. We continue to drag these beliefs along with us, however, repeatedly experiencing situations which reinforce them. We tell ourselves, for example, that our basic clumsiness causes us to drop and break things.

Reality is just a little different. We don't simply fall into situations accidentally, but create them around ourselves based on our beliefs about reality. A man who is embarrassed about his »terrible« clumsiness, for example will so restrict his movements, afraid of being clumsy, that his movements really will be clumsy. Whatever true natural grace he may possess remains undiscovered and undeveloped, because at some time in the past someone convinced him to see himself as clumsy.

If we closely examine aspects of ourselves which are unsatisfactory, we can see that each uncomfortable or unworkable situation serves to show us our own misconceptions and mistaken attitudes. Once we have seen these for what they are, we can correct or let go of them.

Indications: *Free yourself from whatever limits your mind and spirit. But be sure you express your ideas and plans in ways that other people will understand. Accept their opinions humbly. Your thinking may be way ahead of its time, but you can adjust to make your vision workable in the present without sacrificing anything!*

Question: *What beliefs, feelings, relationships or programmed ideas do you allow to limit you?*

Suggestion: *Learn about creative visualization. Read Creative Visualization, a book by Shakti Gawain.** *

Affirmation: *My creative possibilities have no limits.*

---

* Whatever Publishing Company, P.O. Box 137, Mill Valley, CA 94941, UK 1978.

PRINCESS OF SWORDS

Princess of Swords

Key Words: *the earthy aspect of air; out of the clouds into clarity; victory over moods; rebellion.*

The Princess of Swords represents a fresh intellectual clarity which shakes everything up. She has just demolished the old altar, which explodes, sending clouds of smoke, rubble and ash into the air. When intellectual and spiritual (air) renewal meet the element earth, the altars of old ideals are destroyed, and the smoke will soon settle, leaving room for clarity.

Every change, every inner conflict you experience sends smoke and ash (emotions and moods) flying into the air. But the Princess of Swords does not allow the dust, caused by the destruction of the old and useless, to cloud the clarity of her vision! She uses her sword to sweep away moods and disruptive thoughts which arise. She is resolute and aggressive, dealing well with practical issues, particularly when they include contradictory or paradoxical elements.

The Princess of Swords represents an extremely rebellious person who is not to be intimidated either by the established or the sanctified.

Because she rebels in the name of clarity, openness and truth, she is prepared to destroy anything repressive, anything which prevents a full experience life, including all moral codes. Her »no« to repression is rooted in a deep »yes« to herself and existence. We can compare her actions to Jesus' throwing the moneylenders out of the temple.

Indications: *Your thoughts and vision may at times destroy »holy« altars. Don't let yourself be buried by the flying debris. Don't allow your moods to take hold of you. Remain true to your real ideals.*

Questions: *What old »altars« are present in your surroundings, in your life? Have you the courage to destroy them?*

Suggestion: *Look inside, see if your rebellion is rooted in love.*

Affirmation: *My rebellion is positive, constructive and creative.*

KNIGHT OF DISKS

Knight of Disks

Key words: *the fiery aspect of earth; doctor, healer; financial investment; harvest, work and toil.*

The Knight of Disks is a master of health and material abundance. His diagnostic ability can be applied to the body, and also other material realms; money, finance, capital. In questions of health he is valuable in his capacity as a doctor and healer. In financial questions, his advice should be taken.

On the card it is harvest time. The grain in the foreground is ripe. The Knight holds a thresher, he is bringing in the harvest. Harvest means toil as well as abundance. The small, invincible Knight is restricted in his stiff armor. The horse seems exhausted, as if after a long, hard ride. How difficult it is to make the inner wealth outwardly visible, and to harvest the fruits of these efforts!

But the work is well worth the effort, if it is done in the service of personal growth. The Knight's shield is surrounded by concentric circles of sunlight which transform the brown hills in the background into the green of renewed creativity. The stag's head and upturned visor on his helmet emphasize his expanded perception. Spiritual powers are closely bound with the earth and offered in service to her (red-brown cape connects head and earth). The earth lends them form and structure which are necessary in order to implement these powers in dealing with earthy, physical reality. This structure can be all too often experienced as binding by the spirit longing for limitlessness and independence.

The boundless freedom the spirit seeks will not, however, be found in fleeing from the demands of the material realities of the world around us. Freedom develops through our surrender, with love and service, to all dimensions of earthly life.

Indications: *Now is the time to set your abilities to work in service of some kind. The tasks before you are large and demand the use of all your powers. If you make the effort, the harvest will reward you richly.*

Question: *Are there tasks you would like to avoid in your life?*

Suggestion: *Whenever things seem to be too much trouble for you, concentrate on the positive results of your actions for you and for others. Your internal learning and growing process is the most important outcome, more important than that which you achieve by your actions.*

Affirmation: *With every task that comes my way, comes also the energy needed to accomplish it.*

QUEEN OF DISKS

Queen of Disks

Key Words: *the watery aspect of earth; fruitfulness; physical nourishment; overcoming the barren past.*

The Queen of Disks has the long hard way through the desert (background of the card) behind her and has arrived in a greener, more fertile land. She rests, sitting on a huge pineapple, enjoying the refreshing oasis, and takes the time to look back on her long and difficult path.

The crystal-topped staff, and the curled horns on her head, symbolize the clarity of her enhanced powers of perception. Her clothes of reptile skins, and the globe in her arm, symbolize the renewal of the earth and are an indication of fruitfulness.

The he-goat in front of her represents the procreative capacity necessary for new life. He can also be seen as Capricorn: tough, tenacious, independent. The Queen of Disks gives great care to her body. She knows precisely what attention the body needs in order to reflect suitably, as the temple of the Soul, her internal beauty. This applies to physical and cosmetic care as well as good nourishment and care of her health.

Indications: *You have past through an arid stretch on your journey and have now arrived in more fruitful surroundings. Now you can rest and devote some attention to yourself and your physical needs.*

Questions: *In what ways have you neglected your body, your outer self? Do you indulge yourself?*

Suggestion: *Devote more attention to your health and physical beauty than you have until now.*

Affirmation: *I give my body the gift of loving attention, it gives me the gift of life energy, joy in living and health.*

PRINCE OF DISKS

Prince of Disks

Key Words: *the airy aspect of earth; mastery of structure, design, architecture; great energy in dealings with the material; unshakeable; prudence; meditation; physical activity.*

The Prince of Disks represents the process of blooming and pollination, symbolized by the many different flowers behind him. He sits in a solidly built chariot pulled by a powerful bull. The bull symbol is repeated on the Prince's helmet. The fruits surrounding him indicate the richness of the harvest which will follow fertilization and growth.

In his left hand is a globe (the earth) containing mathmatical symbols, a reference to the continually renewed manifestation (fruits) on macro and micro levels of existence. The scepter in his right hand, topped by a ball and cross, represents global consciousness which expresses itself in every earthly manifestation.

The bull draws the chariot with unfailing will. Nothing will stop him, nothing can break his determination to reach the goal. It is particularly in the most important and serious situations that he proves, again and again, that he is unshakable and posseses prudence and perseverance.

The Prince's openness (he is naked and unprotected), combined with the qualities of the bull, make him trustworthy in his dealing with others. The Prince is meditative. In his creative interaction with the earth he comes to a deep understanding of the meaning of life.

Indication: *This is the time to take action; if you do so, important experiences will result.*

Questions: *What activities do you enjoy? What activities would help you toward self-realization?*

Suggestion: *Find a physical creative activity in which you find joy and fulfillment.*

Affirmation: *I am finding the work that fulfills and satisfies me.*

PRINCESS OF DISKS

Princess of Disks

Key Words: *the earthy aspect of earth; pregnancy; Mother Earth; birth, renewal; harmony.*

The Princess of Disk's rounded abdomen is an indication that she is pregnant. This is the third card for motherhood in this Tarot. (See also The Empress and Queen of Cups.) In a broad sense, she can be interpreted as the mother of a new identity, idea or concept.

She holds a disk in her left hand, whose center is the Chinese symbol for perfect balance: yin/yang. From this center of utter balance blooms the rose of the great mother of fertility, Isis. Yin and yang, male and female, in harmonic balance, provide the proper environment for all realms of our lives to unfold afresh in a balanced way.

The staff in her right hand extends above the border of the painting into the heavens and bears a light-radiating crystal at the other end. This crystal, or diamond, represents the birth of the highest form of light. This bearer of the light has been created in the earth, darkest of all the elements, and now is able to bring light back to the Earth.

The Princess of Disks wears ram horns on her head. These are a sign of entering into something new. Her hair is drawn into two thick braids, and then falls free again. The braid symbolizes the interlacing of three beings (father, mother, child), which brings obligations and commitment. But this interrelationship is not an end in itself. After the necessary time of commitment, the three, like the hair in the painting, are unbound and flow freely.

The Princess's throne is in a grove of holy trees at the foot of the holy mountains. The earth in which the trees are rooted glows with the sacred yellow light of the spirit, transported from Heaven to Earth through the staff. The trees represent the unifying of spirit with matter. When the new is given birth, the light is brought to Earth. The energy of the cosmos becomes visible through human life and deeds, and that energy impregnates all with its divine quality. The creation which takes place in darkness and stillness will emerge and spread the divine, the light, sharing it once again with the mother who gave it birth.

Indication: *Something new is entering your life. Prepare yourself!*

Question: *What must you do in order to be ready for something new to come into your life?*

Suggestion: *Meditate a while with the picture of the Princess. Breathe gently, letting your eyes rest on the yin-yang symbol. Then close your eyes and feel the quality of newness now entering your life.*

Affirmation: *I am now ready for the new beauty in my life.*

THE
MINOR ARCANA

ACE OF WANDS

Ace of Wands

Key Words: *fire; high or strong energy; transformation.*

The Ace of Wands is represented by a huge flaming torch, symbol of the element fire, which rules Wands. This is the second highest energy card (the Sun is the highest) in the deck. This card shows the energies which arise after all blocks have been removed. The bolts of light go off in all directions, representing the power bursting out of these flames. All security and certainties you have been clinging to will be shaken and destroyed by the impact of the energies breaking through.

If all obstacles are out of the way, renewal in all areas and levels of life take place. The revitalizing power fills your entire being with new light. Now it is important for the free-flowing energies to have a creative outlet. You can use the energy only if you have a goal toward which you can direct it. The next step, after releasing the blocks, is to find the right framework in which to set this energy to work.

Indication: *You are full of power and energy! Engage fully in discovering where and how you can and want to use it!*

Questions: *What attracts you (to doing it) the most? What gives you the most pleasure? In what framework could you realize your dreams?*

Suggestion: *Draw cards for the above questions.*

Affirmation: *I express my energy and power openly.*

TWO OF WANDS – DOMINION

Key Words: *Mars in Aries; warlike energy; the dynamic pioneer; domination or mastering the situation.*

The planet Mars, bearer of dynamic active powers, is in his own sign Aries, the pioneer who constantly seeks new ways and methods of advancement. The drive forward finds new directions.

The wands are represented by two crossed dorjes, the Tibetan symbol of the thunder-clap. The masks, with horses' heads at the ends of the wands, are symbols of pure destructive energy. The arrowheads are ornamented with snakes. This indicates the renewal which accompanies destruction.

Dominion rests on harmony and centeredness. A better expression might be »command« in the sense of having command of yourself as well. This condition demands that your energies are collected and concentrated to provide the courage necessary to embark on new paths. Whatever drastic changes may occur along the way, the pioneer will not be thrown off balance.

The background of the painting shows the meetings of fire and water, an alchemical symbol of the unification of differing aspects of our being. Out of this union arises the new. When you accept differences and apparent conflicts, solutions become possible which change and increase your perspective.

Indications: *Pay attention to centering. If you're in contact with your center, you are certain to master the situation. Trust your energy. Don't go for any false compromises!*

Question: *Which tasks and situations are a challenge to you?*

Suggestion: *If you are in a challenging situation, sit down upright and comfortably. Breathe deeply into your abdomen. Wait until your breathing flows gently and calmly and you feel quite relaxed. Now visualize the situation at hand. See yourself dealing with it while remaining centered.*

Affirmation: *I find the strength I need now in my center.*

THREE OF WANDS – VIRTUE

Key Words: *Sun in Aries; virtue, integrity, honesty, self-confidence, no compromises.*

The three wands bear lotus blossoms which are in the process of opening. This blossoming is the result of an inner awakening. Body, intellect, and spirit are in harmony. Out of this state an integrity crystallizes which allows for no lazy compromises. You perceive and allow your own power free play, never giving it over to someone else in an attitude of subjugation. Despite external dynamism, the center remains untouched and clear.

Reflection on this point of internal stillness alows a new sense of self-confidence to come into being, and guards against an overload of unnecessary problems. The wisdom within is strong enough to repulse any anxieties and doubts which may arise. The brooding, analytical considerations of the intellectual mind don't stand a chance when you are filled with life-energy and a sense of vitality (the color orange).

Indications: *Pay attention to your own point and internal stillness. Center yourself and overcome.*

Questions: *Are there any reasons for self-doubt? Do you yet doubt your virtues?*

Suggestion: *If you are not centered and feel doubts lingering within, draw a card to clarify the issue that still needs work.*

Affirmation: *I have the power and virtue to reflect and know.*

FOUR OF WANDS – COMPLETION

Key Words: *Venus in Aries; completion; unity; possibility of new beginnings.*

The circle is full. All contradictions and opposites come together and connect at the center. The harmony between male and female, active and passive (ram and dove) has returned. The fire of creativity is kindled by this occurence.

Venus, symbol of beauty and love, combines with Aries, the principle of new beginnings. The heart pushes forth and seeks the development of the beautiful in new directions. Before the new can arise, the old must be complete. The conflict between opposites must be resolved in a way which will further you on the way toward your highest goal. Tension in relationships can work positively when the individuality of each partner is recognized and respected. This makes it possible for you to support one another in moving forwards.

Indications: *Something beautiful is making its way into your relationships. You may notice it first as established conditions are called into question and discussed openly. Clarifying the old is a prerequisite for a new oneness, a new beginning.*

Questions: *Are you prepared to accept your partner as s/he is in spite of your differences? What areas are in urgent need of clarification or resolution?*

Suggestion: *If there is some tension between you and someone else, now is a good time to clarify and resolve the interaction and complete the old.*

Affirmation: *Completing the old frees me for the new.*

FIVE OF WANDS – STRIFE

Key Words: *Saturn in Leo; restriction; unfulfilled desire; embittered; fearful; vain striving.*

The central wand has become as heavy as lead. The winged disk which normally would indicate an upward swing into higher spheres now bears a star pointed downward. The center of the star is covered by five small overlapping disks. The eye of Horus has lost its clarity of vision. The serpents of regeneration look sluggish and sleepy. The phoenix heads are turned away from each other, as if to avoid one another.

This card signifies a general condition in which the creative power of the Lion is blocked (Saturn). Because the free flow of energy is greatly restricted, it has begun to stagnate. This concentrated charge of energy strives vainly to find a possibility for expression. Life becomes a burden. The tiny wings at the bottom of the staff continue to struggle, attempting to lift the leaden weight.

Indications: *In this situation, the danger of resigning yourself is great. Saturn reminds us that all things must be taken care of step by step. Don't let yourself be overwhelmed. Always look again to the flames behind the wand which burn on despite impediments. When you draw this card, it is a sign that you are ready to face the situation and do something about it.*

Questions: *What insurmountable obstacles seem to stand between you and the realization of your goals? How does the mountain of duties and tasks which stands before you look right now?*

Suggestion: *Go step by step! Take everything a little easier. Draw another card for this.*

Affirmation: *I am more and more capable now of expressing my feelings and my creativity in my work.*

SIX OF WANDS – VICTORY

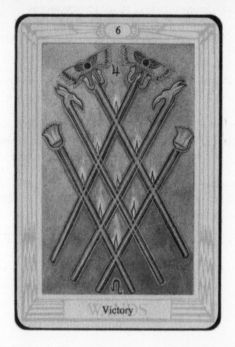

Key Words: *Jupiter in Leo; victory, success; clarity; breakthrough; unification of energies.*

If we have sought long enough (Five of Wands), if we have put out every effort possible, the sudden breakthrough comes, and the unexpected victory is ours. We are filled with an exalted feeling of strength which aids us to victory on all levels we wish for.

The six wands of power are harmoniously arranged, and organized in their effect. The lotus blossoms (love), the phoenix heads (rebirth, renewal) and the winged globes with snakes (creative power, new creation, eye of Horus) are unified and strengthen one another. The flames burn once again.

The violet in the background has become lighter through the secure feeling of victory. In ancient Egypt, this was the color which represented the breakthrough to victory.

Jupiter, the planet of luck and expansion, binds itself with the creativity of Leo. All goals will be easily reached. But the victory should never be achieved at the expense of others, or unjustly set them at a disadvantage. The struggle must be won by fair means, and should be put to the service of some good cause which benefits all involved.

Indication: *Do what you are planning to do. The moment promises success.*

Questions: *What do you really want to achieve? What does Victory mean to you?*

Suggestions: *Draw cards for the above questions. Allow clear answers to arise in you. Then draw another card to show you what supports or what hinders you on the way to victory.*

Affirmation: *I am now ready to enjoy success in my life. Every event in my life brings me closer to my final goal, and my victory brings benefits to all involved.*

SEVEN OF WANDS – VALOUR

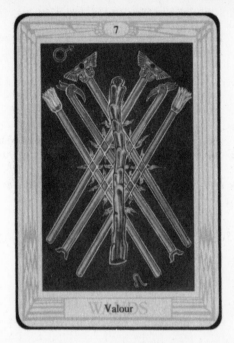

Key Words: *Mars in Leo; courage, daring; impact; taking risks; no compromises.*

The male, warlike power of Mars combined with the daring of the lion produces incredible force and impact. The fight will be carried out impeccably. The violet in the background has become darker (compare with Six of Wands), and is now the color of the warrior who strikes without wavering and is satisfied only with a decisive victory.

The six wands in the background bear the Tibetan symbols for energy. They serve the powerful staff in the center, their energies united and directed toward the goal.

The Seven of Wands expresses an intensification of the conditions represented in the two previous cards. The valour expressed here is an outgrowth of your personal experience. It has arisen through your ability to learn from past experience. If you apply these lessons, you will be able to take further risks with greater awareness.

Compromises are out of the question now: they would require a denial of your own inner reality. It is time for you to stand your ground, and to remain true to your energies unconditionally!

Indication: *Being true to yourself includes standing up for your own truth even in the face of immense resistance. Trust your power. In this present situation, you must assert yourself at all costs.*

Question: *Are you ready to accept all consequences? Become aware of whatever fears have prevented you until now from asserting yourself.*

Suggestion: *Study Don Juan's description of an impeccable warrior in Carlos Castaneda's* Journey to Ixtlan.*

Affirmation: *I express my own reality openly and honestly.*

* Simon and Schuster, N.Y., N.Y.

EIGHT OF WANDS – SWIFTNESS

Key Words: *Mercury in Sagittarius; clear, direct, swift communication; overcoming misunderstanding.*

»Swiftness« is the card for overcoming the hindrances which stand in our way (as shown on the Five of Wands). The blockage, represented by the square, transforms itself now into a large polished crystal, shimmering with the colors of the rainbow.

If you state your own standpoint openly, directly and clearly, these hindrances can be transformed. Misunderstandings yield to clarity. You have found your own inner center and can present your position with emphasis and openness (red dynamic arrows radiating from center). A problem which has appeared insurmountable until now fades meaninglessly into the background because of your clarity. If you overcome the tendency to hesitate, and are prepared to call disturbing influences by name, you rob them of their power to restrict and hinder you.

The rainbow, a symbol of wholeness, indicates that a process is coming to an end. You look back, realizing that the difficulties of the past have helped to bring the learning process to completion.

Indications: *The moment has come for you to define where you stand. If you are open and remain centered, misunderstandings will be cleared.*

Question: *Is there anyone to whom you do not dare to openly state where you stand?*

Suggestion: *Use this opportunity to open yourself up more to those people who mean something to you. Talk to them, or write letters.*

Affirmation: *My openness and self-confidence opens the hearts of those I love.*

NINE OF WANDS – STRENGTH

Key Words: *Sun in Sagittarius; power gained through unifying conscious and unconscious energies; wholeness.*

The strong wand in the center connects the sun and moon. Hidden unconscious powers (Moon) become visible through the radiant light of the conscious (Sun). Latent powers are awakened and can be applied toward a purpose. Recognizing these unused potentials sets free more energies which are experienced as new and unusual. It is a strength that grows from within, symbolized through the crescent moons on the eight arrows in the background. The force of this new-found strength banishes the darkness of ignorance.

When the unconscious becomes visible, we are faced with many things we have covered up in order to avoid looking at them. This can produce fear of some sort, the fear of feeling painful wounds we've covered up and hoped to forget. There may also simply be fear of our own yet unproven strength which reaches into all areas of our lives, reorganizing them.

This budding self-realization allows no return to the familiar situation of weakness or ignorance. Your inner strength will grow with the size of the task at hand. You will experience your energy as going far beyond the boundaries you thought existed. This is a key experience, the beginning of a far-reaching inner and outer unfolding of your potential.

Indications: *You are in the process of discovering your real strength. Trust your inner guide! You may want to take part in groups which can help you develop and unfold your potential.*

Questions: *Are you a little afraid of your own strength? In what areas in your life does this fear come up?*

Suggestion: *Pay attention to your dreams at this time.*

Affirmation: *I know more and more clearly who I am. This recognition leads to the full development of my potential strength.*

TEN OF WANDS – OPPRESSION

Oppression

Key Words: *Saturn in Sagittarius; repressed feelings; energy held back; parting, isolation, aggression.*

The vital energy of the eight wands in the background is repressed and hindered by the two strong wands in the foreground which carry the same symbols that appear on the Two of Wands. On that card, however, the wands are united and support each other, while these two stand separate, next to one another, building a stark barrier.

Sagittarian readiness to communicate is blocked by Saturn, and strong fear arises. If you fear rejection, disapproval or punishment, you will begin to repress your own impulses. Your strength, your vitality and your life energy cannot be expressed. Repressed, these energies turn into irritation, rage and violence. If this aggression finds no external outlet, you may turn it inward on yourself, and it may express itself as self-denigration or depression in all its aspects, up to, and including, illness.

This card is an invitation. Recognize and end your repression and restriction of your own life impulses. This is a step toward taking responsibility for yourself, and freeing yourself from unjustifiable »moral« restrictions and limitations.

Indication: *Whether you are consciously repressing yourself or not, recognize that there is much more which you would like to express, experience, enjoy and celebrate. Dare!*

Question: *There are some things you have always wanted to say to certain people. What are those things and who are those people? You can, for the time being just for yourself, express those things right now!*

Suggestion: *Draw another card asking the question: what will my life be like when I am ready to free myself?*

Affirmation: *I have the right to follow my feelings and life-impulses.*

ACE OF CUPS

Ace of Cups

Key Words: *Overflowing love; emotional clarity, deep love of the self; giving and receiving.*

The white lotus is the symbol for love of a giving nature. It forms the base of the cups, which is blue, color of the element Water. Vertically through the cup flows a brilliant energy beam, uniting Earth and Cosmos. The cup is the medium which makes itself available for the coming together of the above and below, inner and outer.

The Ace of Cups is the feminine counterpart to the Ace of Wands; open, receptive, surrendering; bearing the transformatory power of giving love. The upper and lower portions of the painting embody the same quality; below in the emotional realm of water, above in the ethereal sphere of the spirit. As above, so below. That which is internally felt expresses itself externally clearly and openly. Emotional clarity results, emphasized in the painting by its balance and harmony.

The giving of love happens effortlessly. That which continually flows into us from the boundless abundance of the universe radiates outward again by itself, if we remain open and receptive. You can compare it with the flower which exudes its fragrance whether someone comes close to enjoy its perfume or not.

This giving is not dependent on individual, perhaps close people. There is so much to share! All of existence can take part in it. Becoming one with the all-embracing, omnipresent love is such a silent ecstasy, a cosmic orgasm!

Indication: *You are in contact with all-embracing love. It fills you and you can pass it on generously, lavishly, to others!*

Question: *What is your way of expressing love?*

Suggestion: *Let the card work on you for a while. Read the last two paragraphs of the description again, and close your eyes. Feel yourself as an open channel for the divine energy.*

Affirmation: *All-encompassing love fills me and my environment.*

TWO OF CUPS – LOVE

Key Words: *Venus in Cancer; receptive love; happy relationships; emotional exchange.*

If you love yourself, you are attractive to others. Your receptiveness toward yourself prepares you to give yourself totally to someone else. A deep emotional exchange will be possible, a giving and receiving of overflowing love. The union occurs in complete harmony, as symbolized by the entwined fishes. Two lotus blossoms rise out of the mud and bloom. The cups are filled, and overflow, symbolizing the overflowing emotional riches present. This is an image of complete joy and silent ecstasy.

The water is still and the sky clear and blue. Deep joy (yellow) flows into the emotions (water) and the energy of renewal (green) permeates them (compare Two of Swords). Thoughts are free and clear (blue sky). Seen through the eyes of love, the world appears transformed.

Indications: *Your readiness to receive love makes you attractive. Surrender: to yourself, to others, to life!*

Question: *With which persons, in which surroundings can you now share your love?*

Suggestion: *Pay attention to the love coming to you now. Remain open, and let it enter you and go deep inside.*

Affirmation: *There is nothing to do but enjoy what life offers. I am now ready to let into my life the love relationships which will fulfill me.*

THREE OF CUPS – ABUNDANCE

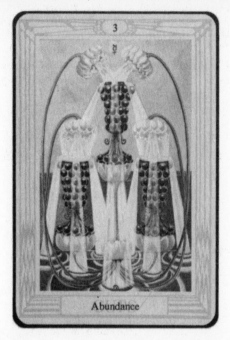

Abundance

Key Words: *Mercury in Cancer; overflowing exchange of love; rare, valuable feelings and perception which can be communicated intimately.*

The three cups are made of pomegranates. This rare and delicious fruit symbolizes the vital treasures inherent in uncommon love. The cups stand on golden lotus blossoms, and golden lotuses fill them to overflowing. Love pours out with overflowing joy.

The love represented here is of the highest order. It is available to be shared with only a small circle of people. The three cups may stand for three important people in your life with whom you can exchange these precious and exquisite feelings with great intimacy.

Such relationships are rare gifts. Care for them with respect and gratitude.

Indication: *You have something especially valuable to share. Be open for the people who can share these exquisite feelings with you. They are also a gift; you don't need to look for them.*

Question: *Are there any people toward whom you have not yet outwardly expressed the love you feel for them?*

Suggestion: *Give whatever you would like to now, in full awareness of your boundless richness.*

Affirmation: *Today life gives me everything I need to be happy.*

FOUR OF CUPS – LUXURY

Key Words: *Moon in Cancer, love, tenderness, care; emotional riches.*

The pink lotus testifies to the love we have received from others. This is part of the emotional richness which fulfills us, expressing itself in our environment through beauty and luxury. The ability to accept this in humility and thankfulness, reveals an inner fullness which can be shared with others.

The golden cups express the wealth of feelings at hand whose roots are deep in the subconscious. This luxury is a responsibility as well as a gift. It demands measured behavior and awareness, as well as an ability to enjoy and share, to pass it on to others.

The danger exists, however, that the emotions take on a life of their own; moderation is thrown to the winds, we are driven by the emotions unconsciously. In this case the clear, pale blue sky darkens and the water loses its still clarity. In times of luxury it is best to be doubly awake. Especially in familiar or intimate relationships an express of devotion and care becomes oppressive.

Indication: *You are being given much love and devotion. Enjoy it without becoming dependent on it.*

Questions: *Are you in any relationship in which you feel restricted? Are you expressively devoted to someone?*

Suggestion: *After answering self-critically the above questions, draw a card to tell you how to deal with the situation.*

Affirmation: *I enjoy being together with (name), full of thankfulness and joy.*

FIVE OF CUPS – DISAPPOINTMENT

Disappointment

Key Words: *Mars in Scorpio; unfulfilled expectations; lost sense of balance; problematic relationships; unexpected disturbances.*

The golden cups have become glasses; they are empty and fragile. The pentagram (five pointed star) points downward, indicating the victory of matter over spirit. A hot wind has uprooted the lotus and wilted the blossoms. The salty water is dead.

The expectations were much too big. Some unexpected event, perhaps only a thoughtless reaction, has ruined them abruptly. The aggressively destructive energies now dominating the scene have probably been smouldering beneath the surface for a long time. You overlooked them, perhaps because you didn't want to admit to their existence. You ignored the warnings of your inner voice, but now you have to face the sobering facts and look them in the eye.

Every disappointment contains, however, the possibility of an important learning experience. The roots of the lotus are coiled in the shape of a butterfly, symbol of transformation, for the caterpillar becomes a butterfly.

Indication: *Either some much too high expectations of yours have been crushed, or somewhere deep inside you lurks the fear of some disappointment. Now is a good time to learn from this situation.*

Questions: *In what areas of your life do you fear disappointment? What have you learned from the disappointments you've experienced until now? How can you prevent disappointment?*

Suggestion: *Draw a card for each of the above questions!*

Affirmation: *I get to know my own reality by learning to see where I fool myself, or deny my inner voice.*

SIX OF CUPS – PLEASURE

Key Words: *Sun in Scorpio; lust, enjoyment; pleasure in sexual relationships; rich exchange of sexual and heart energy; emotional renewal.*

The fear of disappointment (Five of Cups) has been overcome. Body and soul have been purified and are ready for pleasurable interaction with the beloved.

The lotus flowers open, glowing with the powerful yellow-orange color of awakened vitality. The cups are made of copper, the metal of internal healing. Looking closely, one notices the snakes coiled in each cup, symbolizing the transformational power of sex when it is experienced naturally. The overflowing emotions are pouring out of the blossoms into the cups whose bases are made of rare and valuable fruits.

This card is an invitation to give yourself up to the richness of your own emotionality. You may experience this as a jump into water, as the tingling anticipation of diving deeply, of disappearing, of letting go. Rising to the surface, you are refreshed. This is the process of death and rebirth. The result of taking the risk is deep emotional purification and renewal.

Indication: *Enjoy now all which life gives you. This is the best way to express your gratitude.*

Question: *Are you holding on to old beliefs which prevent your enjoyment of pleasure?*

Suggestion: *Enjoy your own emotional wealth and share it with a partner.*

Affirmation: *I am now open to a partner with whom I can share the joys of love on all levels.*

SEVEN OF CUPS – DEBAUCHERY

Key Words: *Venus in Scorpio; overactivity; annoyance; satiety, disgust.*

What a moment ago was a source of lust and enjoyment has lost now its attractiveness. The blossoms let their heads droop and their flavor has become stale. The emotions are out of balance again, and the indication is that some deep disappointment has still not been resolved.

You have tried to cover over old wounds, but the diversionary tactic hasn't helped. After every binge, after every attempt at flight, the leering face of your old problem rises all too clearly before your eyes and colors your experience of the situation gloomier and gloomier.

Indications: *It's time to open your eyes and take a look at (perhaps a painful) reality. Only by perceiving, by recognizing your own inner reality, will you be freed! Every further attempt to avoid it increases the stagnation of your emotional energy.*

Questions: *Is there some disappointment you have not yet worked out? Have you experienced something that was just a little bit too good? Have you overtaxed yourself or overdone things in any way?*

Suggestion: *Draw another card asking the question: How can I change my present situation?*

Affirmation: *As I recognize and accept my shadows, they lose their power.*

EIGHT OF CUPS – INDOLENCE

Key Words: *Saturn in Pisces; stagnation; obstruction, emotional blockage; laziness; unclearness; swamp.*

After the dissolution, debauchery (Seven of Cups) follows indolence. The energy has fizzled out, the handles of the copper cups (compare with Seven of Cups) are broken. Too much pleasure and excessive indulgence!

The water of the emotions stands, not renewed by any spring. It begins to stagnate and the mists of foulness rise to the skies and cloud the light of clarity. The two remaining lotus flowers continue to spill out their energies. But in this situation it's wasted effort. The foul, stagnant water swallows up their small bit of freshness and vitality immediately. It sinks into the sluggish, viscous marsh.

You have already wasted enough of your energy on people who give nothing in return. You have filled them with your energy, but they were like bottomless barrels. You feel empty and sucked dry. This painting speaks of an interpersonal situation in which the river of energy has stagnated. The more you try to revitalize a relationship which has fallen into a rut, the more powerless and empty you will feel. Any attempt to re-energize the other will dissipate your energies further, without achieving any results.

Indications: *It's time you consider yourself, set some limits, and say »No«. It may be an old behavior pattern to always direct your love toward people from whom nothing comes in return. This may be a sign indicating your fears of accepting love.*

Questions: *What people come to mind for you in this context? Are you ready to dare to set limits and stand by them? In what situations do you hide your true feelings?*

Suggestion: *Draw another card to learn what will change when you are able to say »No«.*

Affirmation: *Develop your own affirmation on the basis of the additional cards you have drawn.*

NINE OF CUPS – HAPPINESS

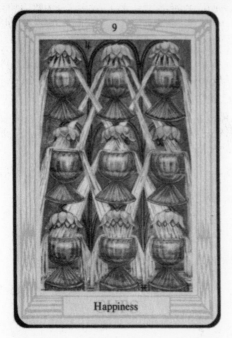

Key Words: *Jupiter in Pisces; bliss; overflowing love; deep joy; blessings.*

The nine cups are symmetrically arranged in the painting. All is harmonic and balanced. An open lotus flower bends over each cup and pours out its energy. The cups are filled and overflow, symbolic of manifold gifts.

The influence of Jupiter in the sign of Pisces creates more than a feeling of mere sympathy. A great sense of blessedness arises from total joy. The quality of this joy shows that it is deeply rooted. It is not the result of some superficial pleasure. It speaks of bliss which derives its energy from the deepest reaches of a soul at peace.

Indication: *This moment is filled with harmony and inner joy: Open yourself to it totally. Don't miss!*

Question: *Where do you seek and where do you find your true happiness?*

Suggestions: *Breathe and feel! If you are alone, enjoy your solitude. If you are together with others, enjoy their presence. If you have a job to do, do it in silent devotion.*

Affirmation: *Happiness is my natural condition.*

TEN OF CUPS – SATIETY

Key Words: *Mars in Pisces; satisfaction, fulfillment; radiating.*

The ten cups are arranged in the form of the Tree of Life. Everything is in its right place in perfectly harmonious order. This is an image of deep fulfillment. The over-sized lotus blossom at the crown of the tree testifies to the wealth of love received which now overflows and pours into all who take part. Everyone who is prepared to receive takes part in this rich river of Love.

The handles of the cups are made of rams' horns. The transformation is complete (gold), and can now combine with the energy of Mars. Mars in the constellation Pisces (spiritual) expresses itself not by being crude, injurious or unruly, but by providing the apparently fragile being with the decisiveness needed to bring forth into the outer world the beauty which it holds deep within. This does not require any dramatic demonstrations of emotion. A fulfilled person simply radiates this quality, and is recognized by the fruits s/he bears.

Indications: *Let things develop by themselves. Everything comes to you at the right moment.*

Question: *What does »satiety« mean for you in this situation?*

Suggestion: *Relax, close your eyes and breathe deeply and calmly. Let a picture arise in you which shows you in a state of complete fulfillment. Repeat this exercise often and connect this feeling more and more with your reality.*

Affirmation: *Life gives me all I need to be happy.*

ACE OF SWORDS

Ace of Swords

Key Words: *Intellectual clarity, original thinking, brilliant powers of thought, divine inspiration.*

On the blade of the green sword is engraved the Greek word for clarity. This is a symbol of creative energy which is brought into being through intellectual clarity. That which is created in clarity will carry this quality visibly and pass it on.

The grip of the sword is comprised of a coiled snake, three sun symbols and two crescent moons. The unconscious (Moon) comes into the light (Sun). The snake, symbol of transformation, shows that the unconscious energies are becoming accessible to the conscious. The energies released in this process are now available to be fully used.

Indications: *Your present clarity is a wonderful condition for your undertaking. You will be able to recognize facts and call by name things which other people would prefer to sweep under the carpet. This entails a great responsibility on your part. Be sure never to express your insights heartlessly. But when you are fully in contact with Love, use your sword without sparing yourself or others.*

Question: *What supports, what hinders your clarity?*

Suggestion: *Meditate on this statement: The truth which you speak has neither past nor future. It is, and that is all it needs to be.**

Affirmation: *I trust my clear perceptions.*

---

* Op. cit. Bach, Richard

TWO OF SWORDS – PEACE

Key Words: *Moon in Libra; inner peace, power to make decisions; Decisions regarding situation or relationships which engender spiritual peace.*

The two swords, symbols of peace, are crossed, piercing the blue-white rose; readiness for love and realization instead of struggle. Deep spiritual peace (yellow) combines with the energies of reorganization (green). This is a condition through which situations can be clarified and decisions made intuitively. Inspiration and ideas which come now are worth paying attention to. Remember them, in order to be able to orient yourself by them in times of doubt and confusion.

The propellor-forms radiating from the rose relate to the airy qualities of the card. They show that freshness and movement also are bound together with true peace.

Indication: *Inner peace is a special gift. Protect it, but never try to cling to it.*

Question: *What areas of your life are especially important to you? You can now come calmly to the necessary decisions.*

Suggestions: *Take the time for deep relaxation! You are in a good position to examine your past, present and future. Write down your insights.*

Affirmation: *Deep peace fills my heart.*

THREE OF SWORDS – SORROW

Key Words: *Saturn in Libra; worries, doubts, lack of clarity, heaviness, depression, tension in three-sided relationships.*

The central sword of clarity is being restricted by the two smaller swords. They are bent, out of harmony. The rose is injured and drops its petals. Clarity has become diffused; gloomy clouds of doubt, fear or worry are limiting mind and soul.

Saturn, a strict teacher, makes all impurities visible, blocks all comfortable avenues of escape. The lesson to be learned here is no less than the mastery of care and worry. A brooding, distrustful outlook must be recognized clearly as negative energy which separates us from our origins.

This card can also relate to a tension-loaded three-sided relationship, and is attempting in some way to explode or destroy it. This situation usually demands clear decisions. Any attempt to avoid making them causes sorrow and worry.

Indication: *This card is a summons to make clear, unequivocal decisions. Only in this way can the lost balance (Libra) be regained.*

Question: *What decisions are difficult for you to make or face?*

Suggestion: *Use the Tarot to reveal what your decisions are (see Systems for Using the Cards). Draw another card now to show what awaits you when you confront your problem.*

Affirmation: *Every problem contains its own solution.*

FOUR OF SWORDS – TRUCE

Key Words: *Jupiter in Libra; calm, centered; clarity; spiritual cleansing; integration; expansion.*

The tips of the four swords, all of equal strength, meet at the center of the full-blown rose. Worries have been conquered. The clarity of the Ace of Swords has been regained, the blue color comes through again. The yellow-green of spiritual creativity dominates the picture once more.

This is a good atmosphere for the rose of recognition to unfold and expand. Jupiter carries the qualities of joy and expansion. Whatever situation has seemed hopeless until now actually contains within itself all the elements for a fortunate, prosperous solution.

The green cross in the background indicates a complete inner unification; the integration of all four aspects: mind, emotions, body, soul.

A warning is also presented here. Truce does not mean peace. There may be a surface calm which is only maintained by suppressing feelings and impulses. Examine very carefully the possibility that disturbing influences are already present, merely hidden for the moment. By recognizing these in time, you will be able to rob them of their disruptive power.

Indications: *You have enough inner clarity to successfully carry out your plans. Be sure at all times that you feel good about what is happening.*

Question: *What supports or what hinders your clarity?*

Suggestion: *Check your surroundings, and rearrange them to support calm and centeredness.*

Affirmation: *I am at peace within myself.*

FIVE OF SWORDS – DEFEAT

Key Words: *Venus in Aquarius; fear of loss or defeat; fear of painful situations or experiences.*

The five swords are arranged in a pentacle which points downward. Equilibrium is lost. The pentgram standing on its head is outlined by drops of blood. Old wounds have been touched and bleed anew. The swords are curved, i.e., they are injured, out of harmony. Each sword's grip indicates a different aspect of this situation. The fish represents the past, the sleeping snake shows that no renewal is happening, the downward-pointing crown symbolizes lost awareness, the ram's horn shows that new impulses are lacking and nothing will be set in motion, and the seashell expresses the need for protection.

Fear of defeat dominates the moment. It may be connected with relationships or, more generally, with the beginning of something which is of great importance to you. It is the fear of losing control, of experiencing the feeling that everything is slipping out of your hands.

Aquarius is directed toward the future. The challenge is to make room for your own objectivity and clarity (blue border) despite the fear of defeat. The white in the center of the painting represents the bright spirit attempting to break through the power of fear.

Indications: *Drawing this card shows that you are now ready to see your fear of defeat. Fear is irrational in nature, meaning it does not necessarily reflect the real situation. By recognizing this you will set free all those energies which have been bound up in your fear. If you are afraid to see control slipping out of your hands, remember, the feeling that you are in control is an illusion! Seeing, understanding, accepting and letting go of your fear will set you free.*

Question: *What do you associate with the idea of defeat?*

Suggestion: *Write down the answer to the above question, or share the answer with someone you trust. If old wounds are revealed, allow yourself to feel the pain. This is the only way for them to heal.*

Affirmation: *I accept my fear and let it go.*

SIX OF SWORDS – SCIENCE

Key Words: *Mercury in Aquarius; ability to analyse, to unify ideas; all-encompassing vision; all-embracing understanding; objectivity.*

Mercury is one of the greatest gifts for Aquarius. Mercury's ability to analyse brings clarity to perspectives on the future. The perceptions are not only seen and recognized, but can also be effectively communicated now. The most varied ideas and visions meet at one central point. This allows for a new, all-encompassing vision of things which brings the rose of realization into bloom.

The rose and cross in the center of the painting symbolize the secret of scientific truth which repeatedly forces us to break away from outdated models and ways of thinking. This does not in any way confine itself to the world of science. Newly gained realizations also serve to demolish old ruts in personal areas and relationships. The changes that are now necessary should be communicated in such a way that others can hear, understand and accept them.

Indications: *You possess the ability to perceive on different levels and from different perspectives. Your understanding of things unites many different aspects.*

Question: *Where are, and what are the ruts in your life?*

Suggestion: *Trust your insight. Communicate in a way others will understand. Allow the rose to unfold.*

Affirmation: *The rose of recognition blossoms in my heart.*

SEVEN OF SWORDS – FUTILITY

Key Words: *Moon in Aquarius; discouragement, despondency, inconstancy, fears about existence; negative expectations.*

The large sword of clarity is attacked and injured by six smaller swords and loses energy and endurance. The smaller swords, each of which bears a planetary symbol on its hilt, represent the pessimistic thoughts which prevent clear success. Conscious and unconscious (Sun and Moon at either end of the central sword) have traded positions. Gloomy subconscious expectations muddy your insight. A heavy anxiety prevails although in reality everything is going perfectly well.

The discouraging aspects of the six small swords can be explained in the following way:

Neptune: Everything seems to be clouded by a film or veil: I just don't know what I really want.

Venus: But it's just too good to be true.

Mars: I haven't the energy, there's no time, I'm already too old.

Jupiter: That's too much good at once. I could never cope with so much success.

Mercury: But I just can't convey it properly.

Saturn: It's simply too much trouble, and it takes too long.

These literally destructive thoughts need not be taken seriously. The reality is somewhat different from your present perception of it. Soon you will be able to laugh over your own doubts.

Indication: *Your fears have nothing to do with reality! Wake up and see what's really happening!*

Questions: *In what areas of your life do you diminish yourself with your own limited ideas? What are your constricting belief systems?*

Suggestion: *Draw another card asking the question: How will my life look when I drop my doubts?*

Affirmation: *I master all the skills and means needed to achieve that which I long for most deeply.*

EIGHT OF SWORDS – INTERFERENCE

Key Words: *Jupiter in Gemini; problems with endurance; worry from thinking too much; difficulty in making a choice.*

Two strong central swords are crossed by six crooked sabers. You find yourself having to choose between two alternatives of apparently equal merit. You will not come to a decision by reflecting analytically. Your doubt, or fears of making the wrong choice, constantly destroy your inner clarity. You are also lacking endurance, which you will need if you are to clarify this confused situation. No matter where you turn, no satisfactory solution seems to exist. The more you try to unravel the tangled ball of yarn, the tighter the knots become.

Indications: *Let things rest and develop on their own for a while. As long as doubt concerning these decisions remains, don't go for anything new. Jupiter is harbinger of unforeseen and unexpected change for the better. The problem which seems unsolvable now will find its own solution in its own way.*

Question: *What alternatives are you torn between now?*

Suggestion: *Relax and let things develop. Draw cards for the possible alternatives.*

Affirmation: *I am relaxed and trust Life.*

NINE OF SWORDS – CRUELTY

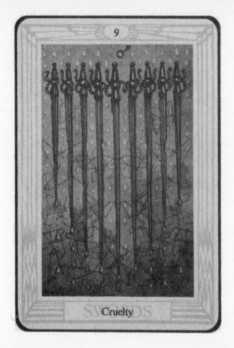

Key Words: *Mars in Gemini; cruelty to yourself; self-accusation, punishing yourself; heartless passion, fanaticism; revenge; passive resistance; martyrdom.*

Nine swords of different lengths hang next to each other pointing downward. They are rusted, chipped and dripping blood from their tips. The tears in the background testify to the great suffering brought about by the swords. Clarity has disintegrated into a pile of rubble.

This card generally means cruelty directed at yourself. It indicates a tendency to »put yourself down« with immense energy (Mars). Destructive accusations made by parents or teachers in your childhood continue, with undiminished harshness, to affect you. But now you, yourself, have taken over the role of accuser.

This may happen in the form of an internal debate between two »people« or points of view. You are afraid to make a definite choice, then denigrate yourself for your indecisiveness. Or you make a choice and then torture yourself with a bad conscience: you chose wrong. The examples are endless, and you will find your own that fit the situation. You feel you are a victim of circumstances, and perhaps you find a bit of satisfaction in this role.

In rare cases, this card may indicate physical or psychological cruelty by some heartless person. This may be a fanatic or vengeful tyrant of some kind.

Indications: *This card points out your tendency to put yourself down cruelly. You will have to recognize and fully see this behavior pattern before you will be able to overcome it.*

Questions: *Who judged you earlier? How do you now condemn yourself? Are you ready now to forgive your parents, others, and yourself?*

Suggestion: *Draw another card to see how your life will look when you accept yourself as you are!*

Affirmation: *I am loved, simply because I am the way I am.*

TEN OF SWORDS – RUIN

Key Words: *Sun and Moon in Gemini; fear of insanity; broken heart; fear of the destructive energy of accumulated anger; negative thinking.*

Nine of swords direct their superior aggressive force from all directions at once against a tenth, and destroy it completely. This tenth sword bears the symbols of the sund and the heart.

This card shows the destructive power of constant negative thinking. It is an image of insanity, a confused uproar of soulless mechanisms. Even the last remains of joy of life (Sun), love for yourself and others, as well as existence (heart) threaten to fall prey to this negativity. Negativity disrupts and destroys the soul's striving toward harmony and balance.

The situation is also a threat to your external conditions. This may make financial ruin, or the loss of other meaningful possessions or possible needs.

Indications: *The first step is to recognize your fear of insanity and ruin. The second step is to understand the negative energy which lies hidden behind your fear. If you want to, you can vanquish this fear by recognizing it.*

Questions: *What are your greatest fears? How would the total destruction of your life look?*

Suggestion: *Once you have recognized in what areas your fears lie, formulate your own specific affirmations, using only positive terms, to help you »reprogram« yourself.*

Affirmation: *I invite the positive into my life, and welcome it wholeheartedly.*

ACE OF DISKS

Ace of Disks

Key Words: *Inner and outer richness; great success; unification of the body and soul, material and spirit, heaven and earth; wholeness.*

The symbols of the card are arranged in the form of a cross representing the integration of the vertical and horizontal, the inner and the outer.

Body and soul, too long set at odds, meet now in harmonic union. Now the body can be treated as the living temple of the soul. The more deeply we are grounded in our bodies, the fewer difficulties will arise during this integration process. The deeper our roots reach into the earth, the higher the soul will be able to soar.

A seven pointed star and two pentangles surround the esoteric symbol 1/666 which represents completion. TO META OPHION means initiation or entrance. Intended here is the possiblity of our entrance into a new consciousness and readiness for a life which is externally and internally rich.

This new consciousness brings with it an attitude of continual development, symbolized by the »age rings« on the wood. New levels of being are continually being reached, like concentric arches. Each in its turn is discovered, accepted, integrated, and brought toward external expression, like the rings of a tree. This process leads to a real consciousness of the self, a basis for real success.

Some teachers will tell us that we can be both inwardly and outwardly rich, that it is not necessary to chose between the two. The inner life is not against the outer. It is important to understand what inner and outer richness really means. Many teachers will tell you about this, for if a student is to ever become wholly conscious you must understand that the outward trappings of poverty do not mean that you are inwardly more aware. The concept and poverty only means that you are not »clinging« to money to obtain it. Poverty means that you do not own anything – including your memories. However, you can »use« anything you wish.

Once you realize this, you can continue to grow on an inner level, and you can attain the highest consciousness possible.

Indications: *The Ace of Disks mirrors your readiness to live a life that is inwardly and outwardly rich. All that is needed is already at hand. Give yourself up to the fullness of life, and learn to use your wings.*

Question: *What areas of your life would you like to make richer?*

Suggestion: *Work intensively on discovering and developing your potential, your inner wealth. Remain open for every form of enrichment in your life.*

Affirmation: *Wealth is my natural condition. It allows me to express my spirituality and creative potential in this world.*

TWO OF DISKS – CHANGE

Key Words: *Jupiter in Capricorn; change, transformation.*

A huge snake, symbol for infinity. This signifies perpetual change. The snake encloses two disks, the Chinese yin/yang, symbols of balance and harmony. They turn in opposite directions, representing internal and external change. The triangles, which are ancient alchemical symbols, are painted in the colors of the four elements; red for fire, blue for water, grey for for earth and yellow for air. The transformation touches all realms of being.

Jupiter, the planet symbolizing luck and expansion, indicates that the change will bring luck and enrich life. The new will bring more stability and security (Capricorn) with it.

Change is always necessary when the old falls out of equilibrium. Changes shake us and wake us up. The crown on the snake's head is a symbol of wakefulness.

The violet color (color of the warrior) shows that new energies will be drawn from the transformation. The only permanent thing is impermanence. The only certain thing is uncertainty.

Indication: *Your life is subject to a constant change which allows you to grow, extending and expanding you, untimately enriching you. Give yourself up to the transformation with trust!*

Questions: *What internal or external changes are going on in your life? Where are you still clinging?*

Suggestion: Meditate on the statement: The only constant thing is change.

Affirmation: *Every day, in every way, I am getting better and better.*

THREE OF DISKS – WORK

Key Words: *Mars in Capricorn; work, toil; gradual progress; duty to oneself; self-confidence.*

This card indicates full employment of your energies in any situation which you feel yourself obliged to deal with. You are willing to undertake even difficult tasks: the sense of obligation comes from within.

Your whole being is needed: full engagement of all your energy is necessary now. The three wheels symbolize body, mind and spirit. None of these three can be left out. Only through their combined and balanced use will you see visible results (the crystal pyramid). The energies of different planes are united by their common goal.

Clarity arises (crystal). The heavens begin to open. The clouds of uncertainty may repeatedly blur your clear vision of the goal. But your unshakable affirmation of the work you have begun gives you the power to overcome temporary doubts. This assures your gradual progress.

Indication: *Some situation is demanding your readiness to work steadily. Engage yourself totally, it's worth it!*

Questions: *In what areas do you still hold yourself back? In which areas could you be giving more of your energies?*

Suggestion: *Find out, and remain aware of, what you want to set your full energies toward achieving.*

Affirmation: *I am now ready to give everything and receive everything.*

FOUR OF DISKS – POWER

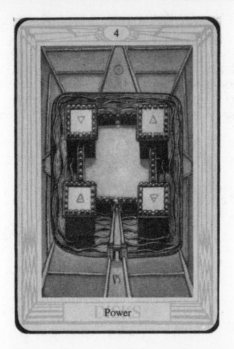

Key Words: *Sun in Capricorn; manifestation; integrity, character.*

The four disks are set in a square representing the four corner towers of a fort. Each bears the sign of an alchemical element. This formation symbolizes security and strength on all levels of being. The power expressed in the card is shown in the solid, almost rigid form of the building. Everything is in its place. No superfluous ornaments decorate the fortress walls.

This submission to a prescribed order has both positive and negative aspects. Such a compact, closed system, with visible boundaries and solid standards, provides certain advantages. A person with such attributes has character, is someone to depend on. Such a person remains unshakably true to personal principles and conducts all dealings with absolute integrity. This is the rare person who lives out his or her ideals.

Another possible meaning is crystallization, holding rigidly to the letter of the law, becoming a stickler, crusading for one's principles. One's guidelines and commandments take on a life of their own and upholding the standards seems more important than being vital and human. Natural impulses are suppressed in order not to compromise one's character. Cold, stiff politeness replaces real warmth and friendship.

Indication: *The meaning of the card depends on the background of the person who draws it. The card can be an admonishment indicating a need to become more established in one's character and integrity. Or, it could be a challenge to submit one's rules and principles to life and the impulses of the heart.*

Question: *Is your life, your behavior, like a rigid fort? Or does your life, your behavior need more order, structure, and solidity?*

Suggestion: *Study the different aspects of power.*

Affirmation: *I offer my power in the service of love.*

FIVE OF DISKS – WORRY

Key Words: *Mercury in Taurus; cares; brooding; pessimism; survival fears; problematic communication.*

The pentagram (five-pointed star) has fallen out of balance. Its tip points downward. Some situation is in a rut or loaded with tension. Clarifying communication looks impossible, so everything seems even gloomier, even more hopeless. Relationships threaten to break apart. Everything dissolves at your touch, and you seem to be condemned to observe while everything around you falls apart. The symbols on the five disks can be explained this way:

Red triangle: your own energy is blocked.

Yellow triangle: your thoughts keep revolving around finding a solution, a way out, a breakthrough.

Light blue crescent: the situation touches the depths of your subconscious. It goes right through you.

Black oval: black hole, no way out, hopelessness.

Blue circle: your inner wisdom admonishes you to do something. The problem in this situation is that you remain idle while at the same time tormenting yourself with your entangled thoughts.

Indications: *When you've drawn this card, you are ready to look at your situation as it is. You now have an opportunity to free yourself by initiating the necessary discussion (either with partners or with yourself). Only clear and open communication will facilitate progress.*

Questions: *In what areas or situations are you not clear and decisive enough? With which people do you need to clarify things?*

Suggestion: *Draw another card to see what will change when you have an open discussion or allow yourself to look bravely at the truth of the situation.*

Affirmation: *I am straightening out my life.*

SIX OF DISKS – SUCCESS

Key Words: *Moon in Taurus; external manifestation of the inner; success, transformation.*

A meditation card for undertakings of each and every kind! From a deep subconscious level of your being (moon) springs an urge for external expression. The cross with the lotus flower in the center symbolizes this process. The internal, represented by the cross in the background, unfolds itself and blossoms visibly.

The six planets, representing internal processes, circle in harmonic order and promise luck and success. Each gives important clues which, when attended to, assure the successful outcome of any enterprise.

Saturn: Success comes to those who go carefully, step by step. Examine and scrutinze everything carefully. Above all, the beginning and end of an enterprise must be planned and thought out to the last detail.

Jupiter: It is much too trying and boring to go step by step through every phase of a process. Be open also to taking risks. Be open for wonderful surprises and sudden changes or expansion. This demands flexibility and openness to new, unexpected developments.

Venus: Success also involves strong emotional energy. Only if you are open to the deep dimensions of feeling will you be able to fully enjoy the happiness of success.

Moon: Success must grow out of the inner depths, and bring something from these depths into view.

Mercury: Success demands effective communication. Ideas must be expressed in ways that touch people and inspire them.

Mars: Success is acheived through enterprise, vitality, goal-directed energy and endurance. Difficulties must be struggled through to victory.

Indications: *Be open to your success. It is no less than a gift you can learn to accept thankfully and humbly. Real success only comes once you have learned to serve. Success under these conditions enriches all levels of your being.*

Question: *What does success mean for you at the moment?*

Suggestion: *Visualize as precisely as possible what your success looks like.*

Affirmation: *My self-acceptance and self-confidence are the keys to real success.*

SEVEN OF DISKS – FAILURE

Key Words: *Saturn in Taurus; restriction, resignation, hesitation; apparently insurmountable obstacles; fear of falling.*

The fear of making mistakes touches business, financial situations, physical conditions and/or health. You see apparently insurmountable obstacles in front of you and believe you will not be able to jump these hurdless with the first try. Terrible images rise up threateningly (seven lead disks of Saturn). You tend to draw back, resigned, and limit your actions to the old and familiar ways of dealing with problems.

The blue-black background, which is reminiscent of peacock feathers, indicates that fears and dread belong to the mental plane, and don't necessarily reflect physical reality. But there is a meaningful connection between the two. Negative expectations are powerful thought-forms which, when nourished (consciously or unconsciously), for a long enough period of time, can actually help create the situation you are afraid of. The same, of course, applies to positive thoughts and expectations.

This card gives you a hint which you need to take seriously. Fear, either conscious or unconscious, is present and now is the time to recognize, perceive, and accept the(se) fear(s). These are necessary steps in overcoming fear, letting it go and creating a more positive motif. Thoughts which affirm life in all its fullness and beauty, along with a positive attitude, create the proper energy to change the unpleasant experiences you expect into joyful events.

Indication: *Your ability to deal with things is blocked by heavy and fearful expectations. You should now look at their content and quality carefully.*

Question: *What areas of your life worry you the most?*

Suggestion: *Write a complete list of your worst expectations. Take a new piece of paper and change each fear into its positive opposite. Keep working with these lists, change them when necessary and decide consciously. Look for someone who will support you in this. Draw another card with the awareness that you can accept and drop fears.*

Affirmation: *I have the courage to believe that all that happens in my life serves for the best.*

EIGHT OF DISKS – PRUDENCE

Key Words: *Sun in Virgo; flowering internal and external richness; wisdom, development, carefulness, prudence.*

The tree unfolds its wealth of blooms. It's a time of flowering that relates to internal and external richness. On all four levels of being long-hidden abilities and possibilities are becoming visible.

The number eight stands for harmony, adjustment, balance (card VIII – Adjustment). As you unfold in equal measure on all levels of being, a deep sense of physic equilibrium develops. This in turn affects your dealings on the material and interpersonal planes.

Particularly at times of multi-faceted flowering, extremes and excesses should be avoided. Internal flowering is a delicate process which occurs in stillness. It is a gift to handle lovingly and with great care. Every bloom on the tree is shielded by a large leaf, a symbol for protection and prudence. Also remember that the tree is just beginning to bloom. It is not the time for harvesting or for giving out the newly developing wealth. In order to maintain the internal balance, special attention must be paid on the external level to clarity, order and beauty.

In the context of beginning an undertaking, this card includes a warning: before making a new start, be sure that health and finances are abundant enough to allow for success.

Indications: *That which is coming into flower in you is of exquisite beauty and delicacy. Provide for it the protection and nourishment it needs. You don't need to force anything! Everything unfolds at the proper time.*

Question: *Are you giving yourself the protection and nourishment you need now for your development?*

Suggestion: *Meditate on the well-known phrase from the Zen tradition: Sitting silently, doing nothing, the Spring comes and the grass grows by itself.*

Affirmation: *I relax and trust Life.*

NINE OF DISKS – GAIN

Key Words: *Venus in Virgo; growth, gain; bonded by love, wisdom, creativity; the more I give the more I receive.*

The three disks in the center symbolize the unification of love (pink), wisdom (blue), and creativity (green). The central binding force is love, whose color is visible through the other two.

In this painting, Frieda Harris portrayed the three-way relationship between herself, Crowley, and his friend Israel Regardie. The six planet symbols bear their three faces.

Crowley's face appears on Saturn and Jupiter. Saturn, the karma planet, influenced his life strongly, causing him to carry out his plans thoroughly, step by step. Regardie's nickname for him was »The King,« and you will note on the symbol for Jupiter, Crowley's head is topped by a crown.

Regardie's head appears on Mars and Mercury, references to his ambition and ability to communicate. These two attributes combined to make him a talented manager.

Harris painted her own face on the Moon and Venus. In Venus she expresses her total devotion to art, as well as her deep love for Crowley. This love moved her to the very depths of her being (Moon).

Despite the tension inherent in this triangle, the three realized their common dream, and for all three the relationship was a great gain.

The highest task life sets for us is to realize ourselves. This happens in carrying out the special tasks assigned to each of us. Retreating from your life's tasks out of fear or a desire to remain »comfortable« means denying yourself. Gain comes from giving willingly and lovingly. Giving in this sense means also giving yourself to the universe; giving yourself fully to Life. The cosmic law of wealth is hereby fulfilled: The more I give the more I receive.

Indications: *If your knowledge and creativity are filled with love, you will gain from all situations in life. The more deeply you are engaged, the more comprehensive your insights will be.*

Question: *Do you know what is the highest goal in your life?*

Suggestion: *Check carefully whether that which you call gain is in full harmony with your ultimate goal.*

Affirmation: *Everything that happens today serves my growth. The more I give, the more I receive.*

TEN OF DISKS – WEALTH

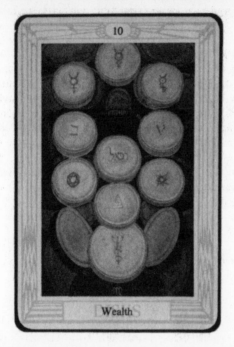

Key Words: *Mercury in Virgo; inner and outer richness; ability to make the inner wealth visible and share it with others.*

The card shows yellow-green coins, each engraved with a symbol related to Mercury. Active Mercury, in combination with the earth-sign Virgo, it is in an excellent position to employ brilliant powers of communication. The origins of any type of wealth lie in human consciousness. If this boundless inner treasure is brought forth into the world, it manifests and is reflected on the material plane.

The ten coins are arranged in the form of the Tree of Life. This indicates that true wealth must touch all levels of your life. Mercury in Virgo represents an overflowing on spiritual, emotional and physical levels. These riches must be shared (communicated), if they are to remain valuable. When hoarded, their energy stagnates and becomes foul. Clinging and grasping arise out of fear (conscious or unconscious) of deficiency, and express a poverty mentality. Even the greatest treasures lose their worth if not used in the service of love. This is represented by the violet coins in the background. Holding back energy which is an expression of wealth turns it sour. The coins have lost their shine.

Indications: *You have attracted to you everyone who is a part of your life. You have created every situation in your life, and you create your own reality. The wealth in your hands is your own to do with what you like. The responsibility is yours, and you are endlessly wealthy!*

Questions: *Do you know about your inner wealth? Do you share it generously?*

Suggestion: *On a piece of paper, write down all the qualities which constitute your inner riches.*

Affirmation: *I am internally and externally rich, and free, and enjoy everything, thankfully and in surrender.*

SYSTEMS FOR USING THE CARDS

The Quality of the Moment

In order to better understand the meaning of the Tarot as an advisor in certain situations in life, we should look at another term first: the quality of time. When we speak of time, we usually refer to it as a quantitative measure: How long has it been? How much time have I? When will it start? But time is not only a matter of quantity, it is a matter of quality as well.

Nowadays few people can imagine what might be meant by the term »the quality of time«, yet in times past the reverse was true. People were very concerned with the quality of time, and almost ignored the matter of quantity. The quality of the moment (a familiar term to astrologers) has nothing to do with amount of time. This term means that each moment or passage of time has a particular quality (or flavor, perhaps) which favors, or even causes, the appropriate events and happenings.*

The systems for using the Tarot are particularly suited for inquiring into the present moment, or viewing it in a new, more revealing light. The present moment is the energy point binding past and future together. Only in this present moment is it possible to resolve situations from the past and set new courses for the future.

Another wise saying which was once common knowledge and has been forgotten is: »Every beginning contains its own ending.« Just as every seed contains a full-grown plant, the moment at which something is begun already contains the entire event, including its outcome. This explains why people in earlier times always carefully sought out the »proper time« for beginning an undertaking. Astrologers were consulted about questions ranging from the proper time to lay the foundations

---

* see Th. Detlefsen, *Challenger and Fate*, Coventure, London

for a new house, to when the next baby should be started to ensure its most auspicious development.

Two of the following systems (Number 2, The Seven-Card Ellipse and Number 3, The Celtic Cross) are particularly well suited for asking about the quality of the moment in relation to personal undertakings. They give general hints for dealing with the situation, as well as exposing strengths and weaknesses to be taken into consideration.

The Tarot cards never bind us to certain interpretations; they mirror our reality at a specific moment in time. It is then up to us to decide how honestly and authentically we apply the message of the cards to our personal situation.

A Word About Mixing the Cards

Mixing the cards is a sort of ritual preparation to give our unconscious mind time to vibrate more and more deeply in harmony with the particular situations or questions we wish to present to the Tarot. Especially when laying out the cards in one of the systems described (as opposed to drawing single cards), you should take the time to deepen your contact with yourself and the cards. The following are general instructions for mixing the cards:

Hold the cards in your hands and close your eyes for a while. Take a few deep breaths, using each outgoing breath to exhale tension and relax yourself more deeply. For just a moment, let go of everything which has occupied your mind until now. Then let your attention return to the question or situation you would like to clarify with the help of the cards. Open your eyes and mix the cards. You can use this activity to help yourself relax and come into contact with your subconscious.

The person asking the questions should mix the cards personally. The process of mixing the cards is an opportunity to concentrate more deeply on the situation. It is possible that you will lay out the cards for someone, in which case you should mix the cards as well. However, I usually feel it is better to restrict myself to guiding the other people to mix and lay out the cards themselves.

The systems that follow are just a beginning in your work with the cards. Have fun!

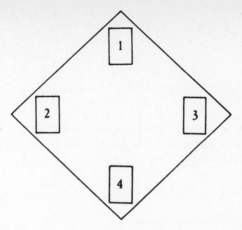

SYSTEM 1:
Clarification of a question or emotional condition.

Mix the cards and set them in front of you in two piles. The pile at your left represents your passive, receptive aspect and the one at your right represents the outgoing, active one.

Mix the left-hand pile again. Lay the top card in position 2 (see Diagram 1), and the bottom card in position 3. Leave all cards face down at the moment. Mix the right hand pile and lay the top card in position 1 and the bottom card in position 4.

Beginning with the card in position 1, turn the cards over and look at them.

The card in *position 1* shows the actual theme which is really of concern to you at the moment. What is really going on? What is the basic question?

The card in *position 2* shows what you are receptive and open to. Which people, energies and events are you attracting?

The card in *position 3* shows what you are expressing and showing of yourself outwardly. What is my effect on others? How do I influence my environment?

The card in *position 4* shows the answer, the key. It points a way in which to overcome the problem actively, or suggests a way around or out of it. Negative cards in this position indicate the possible end of a negative condition or attitude.

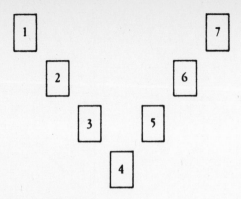

SYSTEM 2: Seven-card ellipse.

The seven-card ellipse is a good system for asking about any type of undertaking. The basic question is, »What is to be done?«

Mix the cards and fan them out face down.
Draw seven cards, keeping them face down.
Mix these seven cards again, then lay them out as shown in figure 2.
Turn them over, one by one.

The cards in the seven positions represent:

1: The past, or that which is in the process of ending.
2: The present.
3: The future, or that which is just beginning.
4: What to do?
5: Helpful or disturbing energies from outside.
6: Greatest hopes or fears.
7: Results or outcome.

Note: You may also draw the cards directly from the fanned out deck and lay them in this pattern.

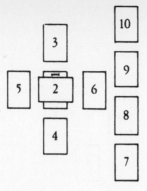

SYSTEM 3: The Celtic Cross

The Celtic Cross, using ten cards, is the most complete system. It gives you insights into the »quality of the moment« from various viewpoints. This variety makes the Celtic Cross an especially good choice in situations involving a turning point in life, for example, birthdays, a change in career or living situation, the end or beginning of a relationship, a project, a journey, etc.

Mix the cards, and cut the deck three times.
Repeat the above two more times.
After making the last cut, instead of combining the three piles again, choose one of them, using your left hand, and mix it again. Using this pile of cards, lay out the cross in the order shown in figure 3. Place the card at the top of the pile in position 1, the next in position 2 and so on.

Turn the cards over and experience them one by one.
Each position has the following significance:

1: Basic card. My basic situation
2: Influences hindering or furthering the basic situation (crossing the basic situation).
3: My conscious thoughts about the question/situation.
4: My unconscious thoughts about the queston/situation.
5: Past influences, or that which is just ending.
6: Future influences, or that which is just beginning.
7: Myself. My attitude and approach to the question or situation.
8: The energies coming to me from the outer world.
9: My hopes and fears.
10: Result, outcome, key.

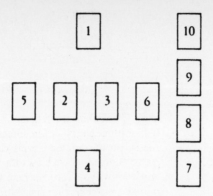

SYSTEM 4: Modified Celtic Cross

This system is especially good for physically oriented people. See diagram 4.

Mix the cards as discussed for the Celtic Cross.
Lay out the cards as shown in figure 4.

  1: Head
  2: Left (passive/receptive) side of the heart.
  3: Right (active) side of the heart.
  4: Stomach
  5: Past
  6: Future
  7: Energy with which I go into the world.
  8: Energy which the world brings to me.
  9: Hopes and fears
10: Results, key, outcome.

SYSTEM 5: Chakra Reading

Chakras are the energy centers through which we draw the waves of life energy from the cosmos. At the same time, these centers are the connecting points through which we maintain contact to other people and our environment on an ethereal level. The chakras are transmitting and receiving centers through which an intensive transfer of energy on all different levels continually takes place. By reading chakras with the help of the Tarot cards, you can see how the seven main centers are functioning, what strengths are available to them, where disturbances are and how they manifest.

The following points will give you some hints in understanding the seven main chakras.

1: Root Chakra: contact to Earth, to the material.
Realms: body, health, money, possessions, forms, colors, etc.
Function: survival, basic life needs.
Position on body: for women, the perineum, for men, the coccyx.

2: Sex Chakra: center of basic energy, element Water.
Realms: sexuality, instinct, attraction, desire, emotionality, impulse.
Function: procreation, perception of other people's feelings.
Position on body: A hand's width under the navel.

3: Solar plexus: element Fire
Realms: power, endurance.
Function: self assurance.
Position on body: area between navel and diaphragm.

4: Heart Chakra: heart, element Air.
Realms: love, surrender, trust, desire for oneness.
Function: union through love.
Position on body: middle of the chest at heart-level.

5: Throat Chakra:
Realms and function: communication, perception of inner voice, expression of »I« energy (ego), clairaudience.
Position on body: throat, under the larynx.

6: Third Eye:
Realms and function: visualization, intuition, extrasensory perception, telepathy, clairvoyance, spiritual awakening.
Position on body: middle of forehead.

7: Crown Chakra:
Realms and function: union with the cosmos, contact through cosmic energies, one with the Universe, cosmic consciousness, manifestation of the divine.
Position on body: crown of the head.

Mix the cards and fan them out face down.
For each chakra, draw one card and lay it in the position indicated in Diagram 5. Leave the cards face down. While drawing each card, concentrate on the area of your body where the chakra is located.
Turn each card face up, one by one, and discover its message.

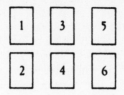

SYSTEM 6: Relationship Tarot

This system is useful in clarifying a relationship between two people when they are both interested in examining what is happening on unconscious levels. This might mean discovering special qualities of the relationship that both have been unaware of, for example. Two partners can play this game in many various situations. Disagreements can be settled, if both partners are prepared to view the question from a new perspective. It is helpful to have a third person there who is also well acquainted with the Tarot.

Mix the cards and fan them out face down.
The partners take turns drawing cards as described below, leaving them face down in the positions shown in Diagram 6.

1: Partner A draws a card to represent Partner B.
2: Partner B draws a card to represent Partner A.
3: Partner A draws a card to represent him/herself.
4: Partner B does the same.
5: Partner A draws a card to represent his/her relationship to B.
6: Partner B does the same.

Turn over the cards one by one, paying attention to your first spontaneous reactions, and talk about the card to your partner. For example: »With this card I say to you...« »I receive from you...«

ALTERNATIVE ENCOUNTER: »I love you, I hate you«

This reading is more lively and immediate than the Relationships reading. The Tarot cards are mixed (both can take part in the mixing) and spread face down between the two partners who sit opposite each other. The two look each other directly in the eyes. Partner A begins by making a personal statement about his or her feelings toward, Partner B, for example, »I love you,« or »I want to live with you,« or »You imprison me,« etc. While making this statement, s/he draws a card from the deck and lays it face down in front of him/herself. The first partner can make three or four statements, drawing a card for each. When everything essential has been said (make notes if remembering the statements is a problem), the cards can be looked at one by one.

Does each card support the statement made, or does it say something completely different? Which statement drew a strong card, which drew a weak one?

The more concrete and honest your statements are, the easier it will be to get at the deeper truth behind each one.

Relationship/Encounter (for small groups)

The relationship readings described on pages 185–186 can also be played by small groups of people.

Example 1: The group sits in a circle, on the floor or around a table. The cards ar spread out in the center. One after the other, each person draws a card to represent him/herself, and each other person in the group. When all have drawn, uncover the cards and share spontaneously with the person concerned what you feel the card says about your relationship. When a card seems problematic, draw another to clarify the question.

Example 2: The group members who would like to clarify their relationships sit opposite each other with the cards spread between them, and proceed as in System 6. The rest of the group sits around them and helps them clarify what is going on. This can be continued as long as there are people who feel they need/want to share something. Mix the cards and replace the ones drawn after the people have clarified their relationship, in order to allow the next people to start fresh.

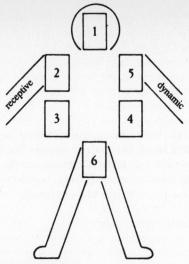

SYSTEM 7: Internal Balancing

Mix the cards and divide them into two piles. Decide which of the two piles is active and which is passive according to your feelings.

Mix the passive pile, concentrating on the passive, receptive inner aspect. Lay the top card in position 2, the bottom in position 3.

Mix the active pile, concentrating on the dynamic inner aspect. Lay the top card in position 5, the bottom in position 4.

Combine the remaining cards and mix again. Fan them out face down. Draw one card for the head (position 1), a second card for the legs (position 6).

Turn the cards up one by one.

1: Head – Communication:
   Positive card: How I present myself to the world.
   Negative card: How I prevent communication.
2: Self-worth; how I accept myself.
3: Which learning processes help me grow internally?
4: How my being appears outwardly.
5: How I deal with the world: my actions, my behavior.
6: Relationships:
   Positive cards: How do I maintain harmonic, fulfilling, satisfying relationships?
   Negative cards: Why my relationships may be dissatisfying or lacking in harmony.

Finding Your Personal Cards

The calculation of the personality card, the soul card and yearly growth card are determined by combining astrology and numerology. Numbers carry specific vibrations and symbols. Based on the date of birth, we can calculate which of the cards of the Major Arcana represent the major themes in a person's life.

The *Personality Card* shows the qualities of the personality which are to be developed. These are the qualities we show openly in the world, the means we use to affect the world around us. This card shows us how we represent ourselves outwardly, what tasks we have to complete in the world, and what challenges to set ourselves.

To calculate your *Personality Card:*
1: Add together the month, day, and year of your birth. For example, if you were born on July 23, 1952, add 7 + 23 + 1952 = 1982.
2: Add the digits of the sum in Step 1 (1982). 1 + 9 + 8 + 2 P 20. Twenty (XX) is your Personality Card. *Note:* If the sum is greater than 22 (e.g., 27), add the digits once again (2 + 7 =9).

The *Soul Card* shows what internal qualities are to be developed. These are the hidden powers with which we find our path, our way to our true self, to the inner master.

To calculate your *Soul Card:*
1: Add the digits of the sum for your Personality Card (20) together. 2 + 0 = 2. Two (II) is your Soul Card. *Note:* If the sum of the Personality Card was greater than 22, and you added the digits again, the Soul Card is the same as the Personality Card.

Exception: When the sum for the Personality Card is 22, The Personality card is The Fool, and the Soul Card is IV (2 + 2 = 4). In the Egyptian Tarot, 22 = 0.

The *Growth Card* shows the energies, tasks, challenges, steps in development, etc., prevalent in any particular year of your life.

To calculate your *Growth Card:*
1: Add the month and day of your birth, plus the year in question (e.g., 7 + 23 + 1988 = 2018).

2: Add the digits of that sum. 2 + 0 + 1 + 8 = 11. Your Growth Card is XI for the year 1988. *Note:* If the sum in Step 2 is higher than 22, add the digits of the sum once more.

All cards are found in the Major Arcana. In this example, XX The Aeon is the Personality Card, II The Priestess is the Soul Card and XI Lust is the Growth Card.

COMMONLY
OCCURING
SYMBOLS

Air: Thoughts, spirit of mental energies.
Bow and Arrow: Goal-oriented, direct
communication.
Bull: Power; energy; fertility.
Butterfly: Transformation (from caterpillar to but
to butterfly); freedom.
Camel: Independence
Colors: Blue – wisdom, mental planes.
Brown – Earth, matter.
Yellow – Spirit, spirituality
Gold – Transformation
Green – Creativity, growth.
Red/Orange – Vitality, life energy, fire.
Violet – In Egyptian mythology, the color of the
warrior; acting without hesitation; uncalculating
warmth, lovingness.
Crab: Loyalty in relationships.
Cross: Union of opposing realms, elements.
Crown: Consciousness, revelation; royal attributes.
Crystal: Clarity.
Cup: Love, love relationships; bearer of the element Water (see Water).
Disks: Coins; bearers of the element Earth (see Earth).
Dove: Innocence, purity; peace
Eagle: King of the Birds; rebirth; freedom; spiritual realization.
Earth: Matter; the body; money.
Egg, with:
wings: Renewal
serpent: The Universe; fruitfulness; creative powers.
Eye: Perception, recognition.
Fire: Energy; vitality; intuition; purification.

Fish: Associated with water (see Water); fertility; death.

Head covering or ornament: Extended perception.

Horse: Youth; energy; sexuality; maleness; soul guide.

Lion: King of Beasts; strength, daring; creativity.

Lotus: Generally seen on cards in the Cups suit (element Water); love; white lotus: love of a giving nature; pink lotus: love of a receptive nature.

Moon: Feminine principle; receptiveness.

Nakedness: Openness, vulnerability, unguardedness; freedom.

Pentagram: Ancient magical sign; when tips point upwards: health, revelation, happiness, luck, harmony; when tips point down: lost balance, unhappiness, spiritual delusion.

Rainbow: Wholeness, completion; harmony: union.

Ram: Power; new beginning; pioneer.

Rose: Usually with cards of the Swords suit: recognition; clarity, truth; wisdom.

Scorpion: Death and rebirth; first rung on the ladder of transformation (scorpion – snake – eagle).

Serpent (reptiles): Transformation; snakes lose their old skins or former appearance.

Sun: Male principle; creative energy.

Swords: Bearers of the element Air (see Air).

Tiger: Fear.

Wands: Bearers of the element Fire (see Fire).

Water: Feelings, emotions; unconscious.

Wings: Embodiment of the non-material; soul.

ABOUT THE AUTHOR

Gerd Ziegler (born February 8, 1951) is a therapist specializing in humanistic and spiritual therapy. Freie Universität, Berlin. He studied psychology, political science, theater and religious studies, at the University, and also worked with encounter groups, gestalt, psychodrama, neo-Reichian bodywork, meditation, etc. He also studied 1976–1978 at the Boyeson Institute in London. In 1979, his path led him to India, where he spent two years studying and living at the Shree Rajneesh Ashram and Rajneesh International University.

In 1982 he initiated a self-discovery and training process *Internal and External Richness*, which has become very popular in German-speaking circles. The focus of this process is to gain access to the limitless possibility which each human being possesses. Ziegler also sees the Tarot as a medium for gaining access, in a playful way, to internal realms which are oftentimes hidden from consciousness. His Tarot courses are a vital and intensive introduction to the world of Tarot symbolism and endless possibilities for helping each of us find our own way. The people who study with Ziegler are open to the widest possible spectrum of experience, covering such experiences as learning and celebrating, letting go and gaining, allowing fear, trust, death and rebirth to manifest. Learning to deal with fear, pain or sorrow can help set us free so we can fulfill deep-seated yearnings and liberate ourselves from subconscious drives.

Gerd Ziegler is available to lead workshops anywhere in the world. He can be contacted through his publishers.